D1030048

WA
AN
CHRISTOPH
EIK SADEEK • A
AN SERTIMA • DENIS
CAMPBELL • JAN CARE
• FRANCIS QUAMINA F RRI
HOPKINSON • PETER KE PADOO • WAL
RENCE WORDSWORTH cANDREW • IA
MARTIN • EDGAR MITTELHOLZER
LE • MOTILALL ROOPLALL MONAR • SH
SEYMOUR • RAJKUMARI SINGH • IVAN VAN
WILLIAMS • NORMAN CAMERON • JOHN CA
AREW • MARTIN CARTER • O. R. DATHO
AMINA FARRIER • WILSON HARRIS • S
R KEMPADOO • WALTER MacART
SWORTH McANDREW • IAN McDON
GAR MI ELHOLZER • CHRISTOPH
OPLA MONAR • SHEIK SADEEK •
H • IVAN VAN SERTIMA • DENIS
OHN CAMPBELL • JAN CAREW
E • FRANCIS QUAMINA FAR
HOPKINSON • PETER KEMPADO
RENCE • WORDSWORTH McANDREW
T MARTIN • EDGAR MITTELHOLZER
MOTILALL ROOPLALL MONAR • F
MOUR • RAJKUMARI SINGH • I
IAMS • NORMAN CAMERON •
ARTIN CARTER • O. R. DATHO
ER • WILSON HARRIS
EW • IAN Mc
HOLZER •
SHEI

Bibliography of literature from Guyana

by Robert E. McDowell

Bibliography
of literature
from Guyana

by Robert E. McDowell

A Sable Publication, 1975

Published by Sable Publishing Corporation
P. O. Box 788
Arlington, Texas 76010

Cover design by Rhonda Boone

Library of Congress Cataloging in Publication Data

McDowell, Robert Eugene, 1928-
    Bibliography of literature from Guyana.

    1. Guyanese literature--Bibliography. 2. Guyana--
History--Bibliography. I. Title.
Z1798.L5M3   [PR9320.M]   016.81'08   75-25786
ISBN 0-914832-03-4

Printed in the United States of America

CONTENTS

CONTENTS

Even before going to the West Indies to engage in research and to teach at the University of Guyana, I was aware that students and scholars experienced the need for bibliographies of literature for the nations of the region. This volume on Guyana is an attempt to fill part of that gap. In the interests of completeness and accuracy, I sent letters to writers living in the country asking for a listing of their works, and took the opportunity in Georgetown to talk with many people who generously gave time to check entries for the bibliography.

This work catalogs some memoirs, histories, newspapers, anthropological studies, and travel books -- especially those titles by earlier writers on Guyana. These inclusions are justified, I think, because early writings about the exploration and settlement of the country, though not always in the realm of *belles lettres*, best explain the complex multi-racial condition of Guyana and the cultural values of her people. This is particularly true of writings which treat Amerindian life, Negro slavery, and East Indian indenture. To state that the present boundaries of Guyana are of recent origin, that the Dutch and English were the two major colonial forces dominating the area, that Guyana is the only English-speaking nation in South America, and that the nation today labels itself the "land of six peoples," hardly begins to suggest the ragged history of Guyana. The evolution of Guyana has, in fact, in varying degrees been determined by Amerindian, Spanish, Dutch, British, North American, French, Portuguese, Chinese, African, and East Indian people. Certainly anyone wishing to trace the origins of the disparate strains of humanity comprising present-day Guyana, and wishing to understand views expressed about the land and the people in contemporary Guyanese literature, must have recourse to such 17th, 18th, and 19th century primary documents as are listed in this bibliography.

WHO IS A GUYANESE WRITER? WHAT IS GUYANESE LITERATURE?

In the case of the earliest writers on Guyana, as well as with many living artists, it is troublesome to reach agreement on who is a Guyanese writer and what is Guyanese literature. For instance, is an Englishman who came to the country in 1850 and spent the last 25 years of his life writing about the country a "Guyanese" writer? On the other hand, is a man who left Guyana in his youth and produced most of his writing in London a "Guyanese" writer? Wilson Harris (born in Guyana) has spent roughly the same number of years living and writing *outside* Guyana as Ian McDonald (born in Trinidad) has spent living and writing *in*

Guyana. So the accident of birth has not been the sole determinant of whether or not a writer has been included here. It can be assumed that the bibliography encompasses work which is Guyanese by virtue of content as well as authorship, especially in the cases of writers who either immigrated to the country or had long residence in Guyana.

PROBLEMS OF PUBLISHING IN GUYANA

This bibliography includes titles of short works -- individual poems, stories, essays, etc. There is justification for listing such brief works when dealing with literature in a nation which has no major publishing house. In Guyana, most authors' short works go uncollected, appearing only in periodicals and newspapers, or they are recorded on tape at radio stations. In another country the same writers might well have found publishers for collections of their works. Many Guyanese writers have in effect produced a "book," but too often it has not been feasible for the authors to compile and publish their works which thus remain scattered about or in manuscript form. Many of the best of Guyana's writers -- and the best are very fine indeed -- have found no alternative to publishing books at their own expense in a nation which provides a small readership and no important presses.

THE ORAL TRADITION

On the other hand, the absence of publishing houses of scope and the lack of book buyers does not completely discourage literary production in Guyana. An oral tradition is still alive in the country. The lateness of arrival of both East Indians and Africans in Guyana goes far to explain this phenomenon. As Raymond T. Smith notes in British Guiana (Oxford U.P., 1964), the steady persistence of African customs and beliefs into the twentieth century was more marked in the three Guianas than anywhere in the British West Indies because of the higher proportion of African-born people there up to the abolition of slavery in 1838. The first boatload of Indians arrived in 1838, and the last immigrant ship carrying East Indian indentured workers arrived in British Guiana in 1917, this late date of entry explaining why much religious and social custom and oral lore from India can be found in Guyana today.

Fully aware of Guyana's rich oral tradition, officials at the National History and Arts Council have drafted an Oral History Program for each of the nation's administrative regions. The Council is now sending researchers into the field to interview older Guyanese citizens and record their remembrances. A bank of such oral material will be valuable in itself; it is also a potential source of inspiration for Guyana's creative writers.

One of the ways in which one discovers the health of the oral tradition is by listening to Georgetown's two radio stations which present folklore, book reviews, serial dramas, and readings of poems, stories and plays, and often follow literary readings with critical commentaries on the works. Much of the literature listed in this bibliography can be found in the libraries of Radio Demerara and the Guyana Broadcasting Service; in many instances the only record of a work is the taped version held by the radio station.

Stage drama is popular in Guyana, as are musicals and reviews. One attending performances at Georgetown's Theatre Guild, or Critchlow Labour College theatre, or the University of Guyana theatre, or even the huge outdoor arena in the National Park, will not find many vacant seats. In addition to the long-standing operation at the Theatre Guild, the Public Service Union Drama Group started in 1974 and presents plays all around the country. And in 1975 Guyana's Minister of Information inaugurated a new West Berbice dramatic group. One of the most interesting cultural activities in Guyana is the annual National and Estates Drama Festival which commenced in 1956 with eleven groups competing. Players perform on sugar estates, in villages, and in townships; the performances are adjudicated, and the audiences remain for the adjudication to verbally agree or disagree with the judges' decisions. Finalists from these groups eventually come into Georgetown to compete at the Theatre Guild. As in the case of radio performances, one finds that more often than not plays performed on stages throughout Guyana are not published; as the bibliography indicates, the majority of these plays exist in typescripts retained by the playwrights.

LIBRARIES IN GEORGETOWN

Most works cited in this bibliography can be located in Georgetown. Finding published works there is primarily a problem of searching the main libraries: The National Library (formerly, Public Free Library), The University of Guyana Library Caribbean Collection, The National Archives, and The Guyana Society reading room library. Several individuals in Georgetown also hold very large private collections of West Indian literature.

Guyana suffered an irreplaceable loss of books when the fire of 23 February 1945 raged through downtown Georgetown, completely destroying, among other structures, the Royal Agricultural and Commercial Society. The Society's library held tens of thousands of volumes -- books, rare serials, unique titles on Guyana.

While the tragic loss of the Society's collection rendered the possibility of study and research less in Guyana, the other libraries, fortunately, were not affected by the fire. The Caribbean Collections at the University and at the National Library are impressive, considering the few years these collections have been growing. To some extent, too, the Society has attempted to build its collection of Guyanese materials in the three decades since the fire, and its small Union of Cultural Clubs collection contains some important volumes.

Concerning the nation's Archives, it is worth quoting a 1911 comment by James Rodway, who was sent to the Archives in order to procure documents which authorities thought might help settle a border dispute with Venezuela:

> "If ever a country neglected its records more than British Guiana it would be hard to find. ...Those of real historical importance were treated as rubbish. At the time I was gathering materials for my history, Sir Charles Bruce engaged me to catalogue the books in the Government Secretary's Office. Some of these were already falling to pieces, and the most valuable, at my suggestion were bound.... But this was a small portion of the documents -- the remainder were stored like bags of rice in a warehouse. When, however, it became necessary to search for evidence ... these bags were taken to two sheds at the back of the Public Buildings and emptied on the floor one at a time. What a mess! Loose books, parcels and documents, and printed papers, all more or less rotted by damp or riddled by insects, were thrown down and trampled on by the unskilled persons deputed to assort them...."

Clearly, the maintenance of the Archives is today as low a governmental priority as it was in Rodway's time. The neglect of the Archives, containing rare books, documents, and newspapers, is a national disgrace. The holdings, stored in an inadequate building (located, fortunately, next to the Stabroek Fire Station), are neither properly catalogued nor organized in any useful way. Most items are rapidly deteriorating in the open air. The importance of the collection of three dozen different area newspapers, some with issues dated as early as 1803, would alone seem argument for moving the Archives to a fire-proof, air-conditioned location where the chances for preserving decaying materials would be greatly improved.

USING THE BIBLIOGRAPHY -- THE ENTRIES

1. *Some general comments on the entries.* Every attempt has been made to reduce the number of items in each entry so as to make using the bibliography as simple as possible. Given adequate information, the following is recorded: author, title, place of publication, publisher's name, date, genre. For journals and anthologies referred to often, the publications are identified in proper alphabetical sequence so that readers can obtain

additional information on the origin and nature of the publications. For titles appearing in anthologies, magazines, and newspapers, only the page number on which the title begins is listed.

2. *Alphabetization*. Articles -- A, An, The -- have been disregarded in the scheme of alphabetization in listing titles. Those authors who use only initials have been listed with the initial of the last name first; these entries are placed at the beginning of the listing for each new letter of the alphabet.

3. *Punctuation*. Titles of book-length works, monographs, television films, radio and stage plays are underlined, while short works -- poems, stories, essays -- are indicated by quotation marks. However, when an asterisk (*) indicates that two or more titles appear in the publication cited, the titles following this asterisk have quotation marks dropped, and the titles are simply separated by slashes (/).

4. *Dual listings*. With single-author collections of poems, stories, essays, and dramas the entire contents of the author's book are listed if the works were available for examination; certain titles from such single-author collections might also appear as separate entries if anthologized elsewhere or if appearing in a journal, etc.

5. *Editors, compilers, pseudonyms*. A cross-listing has been made for all persons who are joint editors and compilers. In case a pseudonym was used for publishing, titles are listed under the author's real name, if known, with cross-reference to the assumed name. Pseudonyms present a challenge to anyone researching literature from Guyana. Even in the competition for a Guyanese national anthem, the winning entry was submitted under a pseudonym. One does not progress far before discovering the Guyanese sense of humor in such *noms de plume* as C. Ranger Gull, Totem Farr, Himself Personally, or A. Chronic Boyle. Particularly in the instance of certain magazines -- but *Caribia* especially -- there were reasons too complex to go into here for writers publishing material under false names. In another case a writer competing for prizes in writing contests sponsored by such publications as *Kaie, Christmas Tide,* or *Chronical Christmas Annual* might simply (in order to avoid public embarrassment) submit an entry under a pen-name, and only confess his identity if he won a *first* prize rather than a second or third. Yet it is not just beginning writers who have used pseudonyms, for most of Guyana's best authors have also published under assumed names.

6. *Journals*. The bibliography lists the more important journals which have included significant offerings by Guyanese. In some instances (*Kaie, Bim,* and *Kyk-Over-Al*) the journals' numbering system has been consecutive instead of by volume, so that reference is made simply to the number and date of the issue, while the volume has been disregarded.

7. *Omissions*. While a few reviews of special interest and sub-
stantial length are included, the bibliography omits mention of
brief reviews, forewards, introductions, and afterwards. Also,
the bibliography generally omits literature composed especially
for children. Several titles for children do appear here, but
they are for the most part anthologies which are compilations of
short works by better-known Guyanese writers, works not composed
solely with children in mind. Some anthologies of Caribbean writing are not included in the bibliography simply because they con-
tain no Guyanese writing.

———————————

   I regret any important omissions from or errors in the bibliography. Every effort was made to make the bibliography accurate
and comprehensive up through Spring 1975, but given limited time
and resources, and given the fact that much important Guyanese
literature has become lost or destroyed or so obscurely located
that it eludes discovery, the bibliography will fall short of all-
inclusiveness. There will show up here, too, the inevitable
shortcomings which accompany a project undertaken for the first
time.

                              --Robert E. McDowell
                              --University of Texas, Arlington

ABBREVIATIONS CODE

Beyond the usual information, the bibliography is descriptive to the extent that each title is identified by genre; there is at the end of each entry in this bibliography one (or more) code letter(s) in parentheses indicating the following:

A   = Autobiography, Memoir

B   = Biography

C   = Cultural, Historical Commentary

Co = Correspondence

Cr = Literary Criticism

D   = Drama

E   = Essay, Speech

F   = Folklore

H   = Humor

I   = Interview

J   = Journal, Magazine

L   = Linguistic, Language Commentary

M   = Miscellany

Mu = Music

N   = Novel

N-e = Excerpt from Novel

P   = Poetry

S   = Short Story, Novella

S-e = Extract from Short Story

Sy = Symposium

T   = Travel

X   = Newspaper

Y   = Anthology containing more than one genre

Z   = Bibliography, Index

* = An asterisk indicates that two or more titles appear in the publication cited; in the case of multiple titles following this asterisk, quotation marks have been dropped, and the titles simply separated by slashes (/).

THE GUYANA NATIONAL BOOKSHELF --
A MINI-HISTORY OF LITERARY GUYANA

What are the first symbols framed to communicate emotion from one mind to another within the national borders of Guyana? The first markings must of course be the timehri engravings found on rocks in different parts of Guyana, representing the record of the Amerindians who first wandered into the area, overflowing into the Caribbean from along the wide basin of the Orinoco, travelling in vast treks from the sources of the high civilizations of the Incas and the Aztecs.

In the wealth of myth and lore which stands at the head of the Amerindian literary tradition comes Amalivaca, whose name appears in some 40,000 square miles of Caribbean legends. One poet has claimed the timehri markings to be the work of the mythical personage who carved upon the Tramen Cliff. He has devised a basis for the markings. For him, they are:

> "Strange figures of maids dancing in the sun
> Shining above them
> These timehri loom today above the shrunken
> river courses
> With the dance frozen still within their limbs
> As that prime artist conjured them -- the virgins
> Leaping in reverent rhythms to the sun
> Blazing his power upon the patient earth
> Husband of all the earth's fertility.
> And with these strange rock signatures he declared
> The idiom of his coming, that he would write
> Upon men's hearts imperishable poetry."

It is always useful to recall our Amerindian traditions and we find them also in the first book to focus the attention of the whole world on "the low lying fabulous country to be found between the Amazon and the Orinoco" (the words of A.R.F. Webber). The book is *The Discoverie of the Beautiful Empire of Guiana* published in 1596 by Sir Walter Ralegh. This Elizabethan courtier described Guiana as a maiden who had not yet lost her maidenhood and he spoke of the fabulous El Dorado and fired the imaginations of his own and later generations. The book was a bestseller translated into all the European languages and into Latin and it sets a fashion in which Guyana becomes the unconscious heroine of a whole range of writing.

There are still extant reproductions of maps prepared by Sir Walter Ralegh showing Guyana the land of waters, in the region between the Amazon and the Orinoco. On parts of the map are written "Here be tigers," and "here be men with heads below their shoulders." This image of headless men carries with it a sense of mindlessness; a man without a head may seek to locate the centre of his individual energy in his loins, and we remember the desire of Caliban to people the island with his progeny. Here is another instance of the dehumanisation of the individual and the reduction of his worth to brawn and bairn which has dogged Caribbean history.

Guyana is the only English-speaking territory in the continent of South America and as part of the extended Amazonian water shed, the colony gradually became known as a paradise of English naturalists looking for flora and fauna of unusual aspect. Missionaries came in order to spread the Christian gospel and many of them reported that the Amerindian tribes finding their way from the Andean mountains and travelling along the track of the Orinoco water-system were the possessors of unusual myths and legends.

Early in the trail of the centuries, the myth of gold, the yellow metal, gave way to the reality of sugar, the brown crystal, and in the sugar plantation system extending from the bottom of the U.S.A. in a broad band across the Caribbean to the top of Brazil, the planting needs of sugar cane called for a surge of population inwards, first from Africa as slaves and then as indentured servants from India, China, Madeira and Indonesia.

This inter-continental movement of forced and semi-free peoples, with their cultural heritage either destroyed or adapting unconsciously to the environmental pressures of a new habitat, exercised a fascination over the minds of the more creative administrators, soldiers and doctors who served the Guyanese community and we find the early literature reflecting this interest as they send letters back home, reporting to their relatives on the bizarre customs, the intriguing marriage of myth and reality, the lisping articulation of new images based upon the old world in the minds of peoples struggling with those of the new world outside their doors.

It is to Martin Buber that I refer for the particular model I desire to fashion in this approach to a mini-history of literary Guyana. He tells us that life is really a matter of meeting, when "I" and "thou" come together on a basis of equality as individuals, and he cautions us against the heresy of looking upon the world as an "I" and "It" grouping when we debase our fellow human beings and look upon them as Objects rather than Subjects in their own right -- as Objects which are customers for our goods, servants in our economy, as colonials in our empire and generally as Objects for our cunning and trickery to work upon. The great and significant movement in any sketch for a literary history of Guyana will be the movement from that of being Objects

described by others from outside the region to that of the stage
when the people of the region themselves begin to talk and write
about themselves as Subjects and the centre of their own enquiry.
This way of describing the creative imagination, to say that
everything in Guyana was considered as an object without sensi-
bility or feeling to be described in the third person singular,
this, of course, was one of the most damaging consequences of
the system of slavery. Where do we find the first evidence of
the Guyanese as Subject and not Object? There is an indication
of the person who may be the first singing voice in our Guyanese
literary history. The first authentic voice from among the
people is a school master at Buxton, who produces in 1838 a poem
about August the First. As we look today at the many competent
attempts to compose poetry, it sounds like the stammering accents
of a child not yet given to speech, but Simon Christian Oliver
wrote twelve lines of verse for the 1st August 1838:

> "Oh! ye first of August freed men who now
> > liberty enjoy
> Salute the day and shout hurrah to Queen Victoria
> On this glad day the galling chains of Slavery
> > were broke
> From off the necks of Afric's sons, who bled beneath
> > its yoke
> With hearts and voice you should rejoice, to God the
> > glory give
> Now freedom is your happy lot, as freed men
> > you should live;
> Your minds you ought to cultivate as well as till
> > the ground
> And virtuous actions imitate wherein true bliss
> > abound,
> To your masters then you'll fill a glass and drink
> > with grateful glee
> And to all those of the same class who nobly set you
> > free.
> Then you should sing God save the Queen, oh may she
> > live for ever
> Great Britain your true friend has been -- forsake
> > you may she never."

Gratitude to the master class "who nobly set you free," filling
a glass to drink with glee, the true friendship of Great Britain--
these are prophetic elements in Oliver's verse, worthy of analysis
and development.

It is to N.E. Cameron in his invaluable anthology of *Guianese
Poetry 1831-1931* that we are indebted for the record of the early
beginnings of an indigenous literature and we select three fig-
ures from the historical past for notice. Thomas Don in 1873
published *Pious Effusions,* a book of 43 poems; Don may himself

have seen slavery first 35 years before he became an author (he tells us that he was old at that time).   His verse shows that he spent his time reading his Bible, converting its episodes into rhymed verse -- the Prodigal Son, the Jailer of Philippi, Christ's entry into Jerusalem and the Destruction of Sodom and Gomorrah.   No less than ten poems end with a vision of paradise and many of the passages are really prayers.

Egbert Martin (Leo) published his *Poetical Works* (1883) and *Local Lyrics* (1888).   He is our first important writer and he had a fine command of images and rhythm.   His range of topics was wide--from the Amerindian in the forest to the royal parsonage.   He sings of children at play and villagers at night entertaining themselves with music of their own making.   He writes of duty, sorrow, joy and solitude and of justice and truth.   For him:

> The poet is a magician
> The philosopher's stone is his
> It turns all baser metals
> To priceless rarities

This mastery of the poet's craft won for him the first prize in a competition open to all poets in the British Empire for the best two additional verses to the British National Anthem and it is reported that Alfred Tennyson was impressed by the quality of his poems.

Between 1920 and 1942 and with a small and perhaps indifferent audience, Walter Mac A. Lawrence poured out a stream of poetry in Guyana in every conceivable metrical form.   A lover of the long rolling music of Swinburne, he composed easily and continuously and he has left Guyanese a major body of work for the national archives.   His poems have a place in every anthology, especially the gems--"Morning," "O beautiful Guyana" and they form a natural link leading to the modern period of literature in Guyana and the Caribbean.

If we move through the more recent decades, we could say that the poets of the 1920s, for example symbolised by Walter Mac A. Lawrence, found that much of their interest lay in the exploration and development of poetic forms, such as the rondeau, villanelle, sonnet and the many varieties of ode.   In the 1930s the poets were swept along by the new freedom to attach subject matter to the literary form and incorporate new strange ideas into the body of verse, shoplists, cigarettes, dance halls and the environment around them previously forbidden or unacceptable. In the 1940s, there was a movement towards the awakening of a political awareness.   Social and political protest developed against living and working conditions in Guyana (as it did in Jamaica) leading to and reflecting the re-grouping of political forces.

In the 1950s, the young poetic voices concentrated on the development of a poetical personality, partly in response to the intense political activity around them. The 1960s threw up another group of writers, in many instances, residents in rural areas who brought in their work images of the flora and fauna of the village and the estate. Many of them were students of the Young National University and introduced the power of ideas into their verse.

Independence came in 1966 and the establishment of the Republic in 1970. The writers of the 1970s find that there are certain new demands being made of them, consciously or unconsciously --to express faith in the future of the country (sobered by the harsh economic realities facing a Third World nation) and to understand the new ideals before the nation and to interpret the past heritage in terms of the new goals.

There will be many answers to the challenges facing the Guyanese creative imagination, but the old themes are still present in slightly adapted forms -- to delve into history and folklore and digest them into poetry; to describe with affection the Guyana rivers and coastlands and its mysterious tree-dominated hinterland; to claim a better share of the national wealth for all, to reject imported standards and to build the sense of pride in the national article and environment; to create a new universe of images and metaphors that express the new sense of personal post-republic worth that will work powerfully in the minds of the people.

The honour roll of fiction in Guyana is a long and worthwhile one. At the head of the tradition stand two novels, one by a stranger and one by an adopted son of the country who had had a long exposure to the Guyanese experience. There is James Rodway's *In Guiana Wilds* published in 1899 and telling the story of a Glasgow clerk who comes to Guyana in search of employment in Georgetown marries a half-Amerindian girl and ends up discovering at Roraima gold coins with the image of Queen Elizabeth stamped upon them.

W.H. Hudson, also a gifted naturalist, is the author of *Green Mansions* (1904) and he concentrated upon the idyllic courtship of the forest-girl Rima who plays with a bird in the deep Guyana forest. For many, Rima is the spirit of Guyana in a simple but passionate embodiment and her olive-skinned Venezuelan lover Abel Guevez is the symbol of the deep attraction she exercises upon individuals from abroad.

Third on our list is the novel *Those that be in Bondage* (1917) by A.R.F. Webber who later became an important figure in Guyanese politics and who also wrote the *Centenary History and Handbook of British Guiana* in 1931. Like Mittelholzer after him, Webber was attracted by the complex picture of life on the sugar plantation but he wrote to prove a political point--the evils of the indenture system, the policy of managers and the abuses of the overseer system and the interplay of morals and human passions. A chivalrous white overseer marries the beautiful daughter of an East Indian immigrant in the face of estate convention and their infant daughter becomes an orphan at the end of a shocking tragedy. Written as a serial and therefore reflecting the shapelessness of impromptu episodes, the novel changes direction and becomes a Caribbean novel. Another theme emerges and the book ends up as the story of a priest disrobing himself dramatically in a Port-of-Spain pulpit. Many themes are here inter-twined -- the attitudes to inter-class and inter-race unions and the dogma of the Church and its influence upon the individual.

These three books are noticed not necessarily for their intrinsic value as compelling novels but because they typify the two poles of existence into which one may attempt to separate the simple classification of a long line of Guyanese novels-- those that deal with coastal scenarios and those that pursue the mysterious attractions of the hinterland.

For the most part, Wilson Harris has staged his books in the hinterland of Guyana and the heartland of the Spirit, but the novels of Jan Carew link life on the coast with life in the interior. The important Kaywana novel-sequence of Edgar Mittelholzer traces the fortunes of a sugar-plantation-owning-family over several centuries on the coastal area of Guyana and in *Sylvia* also he analyses the motives of a coastal community, but at least two of his more successful books are located in the upper reaches of the Berbice River. Peter Kempadoo's main characters work on the coast in our major industries of sugar and rice. These are a few instances but we could go through the list of novels and separate them out into the categories of coast and interior.

It is fascinating to look at the Guyanese novels and to see the way the hidden heroine of them all, the spirit of Guyana is described and caressed in her many guises and roles.

Like God's mercy, the Guyana bookshelf contains a large variety -- poetry, novels, histories, social studies, reports of commissions--indeed wherever a document appears in which a survey of information is put together with a grain of imagination we must read it with interest as an input to the national spirit. We have adventures on the high savannahs, the traditional pursuits of naturalists, the emotions of diamond seekers following a far shout; we have the meticulous analyses of the World Bank Mission. The heroine of our saga, Guyana with the slender waist, has also beckoned over the centuries to a handful of governors with literary flair, like Cecil Clementi, thoughtful magistrates and sheriffs administering the law like Kirke and Des Voeux, doctors and soldiers eager to confide to their note books and letters the unusual customs before their eyes, like Pinckard and St. Clair.

We have a clutch of historians. There is Netscher; I picture him as a pipe-smoking writer of sturdy prose, dreaming back over the lost Dutch plantations, A. R. F. Webber digesting his way through annual oceans of newspapers in order to provide us with his Centenary history in which the meaningful and the trivia lie bedded side by side, Rodway with the careful botanist's approach to facts set out in his large history of British Guiana and the invaluable Story of Georgetown, Clementi signalling to the English reader "the danger involved in the premature grant of representative institutions," and tracing the progress of the country from a commercial adventure, to oligarchy through demagogy, into a constitutional eccentricity that England swept aside to assume the power of governing, there is Allan Young pointing up the interplay of water control, taxation and social services on the coast and the growth of local government patterns.

We find Dwarka Nath and Peter Ruhoman tracing the fortunes of the East Indians, and Clementi chronicling the arrival of the Chinese from a position of far flung interest. P.H. Daly and Vere T. Daly write their histories around people in the heroic singular or in the plural. Bunyan produces a history of the Teachers Association and Harold Lutchman one on the Civil Servants. Guy de Weever writes a small classic for children in his Story of Guyana.

The natural history of Guyana has also its place on the bookshelf. Charles Waterton roamed over this country in the first quarter of the 19th century, followed by the Schomburgk brothers, Robert and Richard, recording life in the 1840s, as they found it, in memorable terms. We must not forget the book *Canoe and Camplife* by Barrington Brown who records his delight and surprise as he is introduced to his first experience of Kaieteur Fall by Amerindians who had lived in its knowledge for generations. There is the emotion of Michael Swan before his ascent of Roraima and as he picks up anecdotes in the marches of El Dorado and reacts to the beautiful song of the Guyana birds, and Zahra Freeth records her impressions of Mackenzie as a foreign enclave in *Run Swiftly Demerara*, while Raymond Smith investigates the Negro Family. Audrey Butt investigates the origins of the Hallelujah religion among the Arecunas. And yet we haven't said it all -- there are the children's books, symbolised by Celeste Dolphin's delightful broadcasts on *The Children of Guyana*. Joy Allsopp's *Teddy the Toucan* on our legends, the stories of Florence Caviglioli, and Gertrude Shaw.

I want to ask two questions. What has been the most powerful application of ideas to Guyanese society in our past, brushing aside the easy myth of gold by hard work? Before the bar of decision come many shadows from the past, crowding upon the page -- Gravesande with a wet towel around his head writing their Mightinesses in Holland in the early morning, distracted by penury, bludgeoned by his son's death but throwing his gaze on to Guyana's future. Robert Victor Evan Wong with his trained engineer's mind, dreaming his dream of using the vast forest potential--to develop wood pulp. Hutchinson, critically evaluating our low coastlands and bringing a dream from India of puting bridles across the mouths of the Mahaica and Mahaicony Rivers to create a certainty of irrigation for coastal crops. In our time we cut a road to Brazil, we dam the Mazaruni for white power, we make an act of possession of our hinterland. We build new cities in the forests, we grow new muscles with nationalisation, we seek to change the images in people's minds.

And finally the last question. Where are the lost Guyana poets, the individuals with creative potential who never had a chance to develop their gift of words?

Looking at the early records for a sign of a truly indigenous speech and seeking the results of the work of the creative imagination in the myths and legends of the Warrau and the Wai-Wais, we must ask whether among the chieftains of our ten tribal nations there had not been some who bore upon them the mark of the creative imagination and who were anonymous and undeveloped.

Among the slaves coming over three centuries into Guyanese plantations, there must have been men and women poets whose spirits rejected the bondage and the lack of worth of the society in which they found themselves. They would have been the leaders of successful and unsuccessful slave rebellions. These slave poets would be ruthlessly repressed and exterminated and their very independence of spirit would have singled them out for repressive measures. We know of Cuffy and his lieutenants in the 1763 rebellion; we know that he was physically bested by one of his subordinates and so killed himself.

In the 1823 Slave Revolt at Mahaica we know of Jackie Reid, the leader with a creative mind, we have the names of Quamina and Jack Gladstone, there is Damon in Essequibo, hanged in 1834 because of his instinctive and accurate belief that the Church of God was not under the realm of the British Crown. And there must be countless un-recorded instances among the Africans, Indians and other peoples, of individuals who came to Guyana, blessed with a creative imagination that brought them into dangerous and destructive conflict with the authorities.

We salute their spirits and express regret that in their

time and generation they did not have the soil which could have nourished their roots and brought their gifts to flower. It is our hope that in the revolution of time this waste of valuable human creative potential will not be repeated; that the social and economic revolutions of our age have gradually made it possible for the peoples who were once in the out-fields of history to achieve a better quality of life, despite what were formerly hindrances of class and colour and race.

-- A.J. Seymour
-- Georgetown, Guyana

ILS
LTE
N McDONAL
CHRISTOPHER NI
EIK SADEEK • A. J.
AN SERTIMA • DENIS W
CAMPBELL • JAN CAREW MAR
FRANCIS QUAMINA FARRIER • WIL
OPKINSON • PETER KEMPADOO • WALTER
WORDSWORTH McANDREW • IAN M
MARTIN • EDGAR MITTELHOLZER
NICOLE • MOTILALL ROOPLALL MONAR • SHE
EYMOUR • RAJKUMARI SINGH • IVAN VAN SEF
LLIAMS • NORMAN CAMERON • JOHN CAM
EW • MARTIN CARTER • O. R. DATHO
INA FARRIER • WILSON HARRIS • SL
KEMPADOO • WALTER MacARTH
ORTH Mc ANDREW • IAN McDONALD
AR MIT LHOLZER • CHRISTOPHER
ONAR • SHEIK SADEEK • A. J. SE
VAN VAN SERTIMA • DENIS WIL
CAMPBELL • JAN CAREW • MA
E • FRANCIS QUAMINA FARRIER
HOPKINSON • PETER KEMPADOO •
RENCE • WORDSWORTH McANDREW •
MARTIN • EDGAR MITTELHOLZER MA
MOTILALL ROOPLALL MONAR
OUR • RAJKUMARI SINGH • IV
MS • NORMAN CAMERON • JO
RTIN CARTER • O. R. DAT
WILSON HARRIS
W • IAN McD
TER

A

Abrams, Ovid. Guyana Mete' Gee. Georgetown: Labour Advocate Job Printing, 1970. (C,F)

Adams, Odel. A Gathering of Thoughts. Georgetown: Magnet Printery, 1974. *Time/Death Bed/Learning/Reality/Regret/ Dreaming/Revenge/Humility/Village Wake/Thinking/Mother Love/ Gathering Freedom Fighters/Lovers, Growing Old/Man, on the Brink/Country Boys, Returning/Reaching Out/Death of the First Born/Visiting Home/Changing Times/God, At Work/Defini- tion of Life/Loneliness/In Memoriam (P)

Adastral. (pseud.) "A Gentleman Jockey," Christmas Tide (1921) p. 37 (S)

Aesop. (pseud.) "The Creative Adventure with the British Commonwealth," Kaie 2 (1966) p. 54 (E)

_____. "Greenheart (A Fable)," Kyk-Over-Al 3 (1946) p. 13 (S)

Agard, B.A. "From Dead Slaves," p. 105 Searwar's Co-Operative Republic (P)

Agard, Clifford. [cf. Ali, Jamal]

Agard, John. "The Cynic," Poet 13, 1 (1972) p. 1 also p. 14 R.C. McAndrew's Plexus (P)

_____. "Do It," Expression 2 (1967) p. 24 (P)

_____. "Does It Matter," Expression 2 (1967) p. 23 (P)

_____. "For Muhammad Ali," Georgetown Sunday Chronicle (3 Nov. 1974) p. 4 (P)

_____. "Frail Things," Expression 3½ (1967) p. 32 (P)

_____. "Haffafoot Jacob," broadcast Guyana Broadcasting Service 1973 (S)

_____. "How Free," Expression I (1966) p. 10 (P)

_____. "Incident," p. 24 R.C. McAndrew's Plexus (P)

_____. "A Man I Didn't Know," Georgetown Sunday Chronicle (27 April 1975) p. 9 (P)

_____. "Mandam Boy Chile," broadcast Guyana Broadcasting Service 1974 (S)

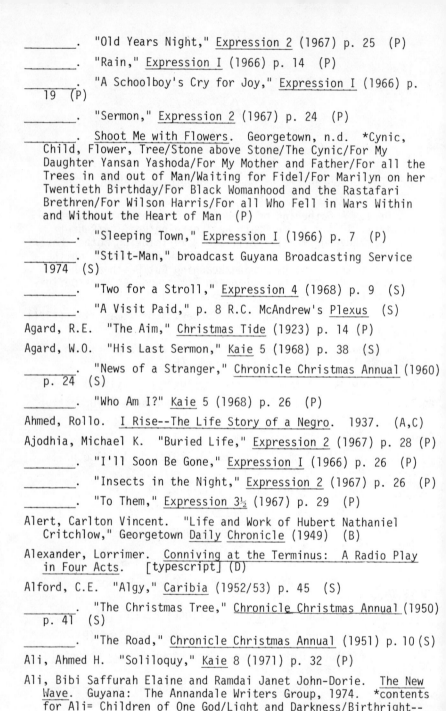

_____. "Old Years Night," Expression 2 (1967) p. 25 (P)

_____. "Rain," Expression I (1966) p. 14 (P)

_____. "A Schoolboy's Cry for Joy," Expression I (1966) p. 19 (P)

_____. "Sermon," Expression 2 (1967) p. 24 (P)

_____. Shoot Me with Flowers. Georgetown, n.d. *Cynic, Child, Flower, Tree/Stone above Stone/The Cynic/For My Daughter Yansan Yashoda/For My Mother and Father/For all the Trees in and out of Man/Waiting for Fidel/For Marilyn on her Twentieth Birthday/For Black Womanhood and the Rastafari Brethren/For Wilson Harris/For all Who Fell in Wars Within and Without the Heart of Man (P)

_____. "Sleeping Town," Expression I (1966) p. 7 (P)

_____. "Stilt-Man," broadcast Guyana Broadcasting Service 1974 (S)

_____. "Two for a Stroll," Expression 4 (1968) p. 9 (S)

_____. "A Visit Paid," p. 8 R.C. McAndrew's Plexus (S)

Agard, R.E. "The Aim," Christmas Tide (1923) p. 14 (P)

Agard, W.O. "His Last Sermon," Kaie 5 (1968) p. 38 (S)

_____. "News of a Stranger," Chronicle Christmas Annual (1960) p. 24 (S)

_____. "Who Am I?" Kaie 5 (1968) p. 26 (P)

Ahmed, Rollo. I Rise--The Life Story of a Negro. 1937. (A,C)

Ajodhia, Michael K. "Buried Life," Expression 2 (1967) p. 28 (P)

_____. "I'll Soon Be Gone," Expression I (1966) p. 26 (P)

_____. "Insects in the Night," Expression 2 (1967) p. 26 (P)

_____. "To Them," Expression 3½ (1967) p. 29 (P)

Alert, Carlton Vincent. "Life and Work of Hubert Nathaniel Critchlow," Georgetown Daily Chronicle (1949) (B)

Alexander, Lorrimer. Conniving at the Terminus: A Radio Play in Four Acts. [typescript] (D)

Alford, C.E. "Algy," Caribia (1952/53) p. 45 (S)

_____. "The Christmas Tree," Chronicle Christmas Annual (1950) p. 41 (S)

_____. "The Road," Chronicle Christmas Annual (1951) p. 10 (S)

Ali, Ahmed H. "Soliloquy," Kaie 8 (1971) p. 32 (P)

Ali, Bibi Saffurah Elaine and Ramdai Janet John-Dorie. The New Wave. Guyana: The Annandale Writers Group, 1974. *contents for Ali= Children of One God/Light and Darkness/Birthright--

Robbed/Portrait of Life/Dreams/Hero of the Morning Glory/Gold
or Not/Heart/Who Be He. contents for John-Dorie= My Pa Pa/
Why/The Cane-Cutter/She/The Beggar/Our Family/If (P)

Ali, Jamal. [Muslim name of Clifford Agard] Black by Night.
perf. London: Oval Theatre 1972 (D)

_____. Black Feet in the Snow. perf. London: Commonwealth
Institute 1973 (D)

_____. "Dimensions of Confusion," Savacou 9/10 (1974)
p. 13 (P)

Alli, Laiquat. "I am a Cane Cutter," Kaie 8 (1971) p. 30 (P)

Allsopp, Joy. "Leafing through Schomburgk," Kyk-Over-Al 26
(1959) p. 31 (E)

_____. "Thinking about Roger Mais," Kyk-Over-Al 24 (1958)
p. 75 (E)

Allsopp, Richard. "British Honduras--the Linguistic Dilemma,"
Caribbean Quarterly 11, 3 and 4 (1965) p. 54 (E)

_____. "The English Language in British Guiana," English
Language Teaching 12, 2 (1958) p. 59 (E)

_____. "Folklore in Guyana--Building a Guyanese Tradition"
Kaie 4 (1967) p. 37 (E)

_____. "The Language We Speak (Part I)," Kyk-Over-Al 9 (1949)
p. 13 (E)

_____. "The Language We Speak (Part IV)," Kyk-Over-Al 17
(1953) p. 235 (E)

_____. "The Language We Speak--Letter to Frank Collymore,"
Kyk-Over-Al 16 (1953) p. 127 (E)

_____. "Some Problems in the Lexicography of Caribbean
English," Caribbean Quarterly 17, 2 (1971) p. 10 (E)

_____. "What Dictionary Should West Indians Use?" Journal
of Commonwealth Literature 6 (1971) p. 133 (E)

_____. [cf. Seymour, A.J.--"Standards of Criticism," and
"The Literary Tradition in Guyana"]

Alton, Steve. "Hero Play," Christmas Tide (1934) p. 51 (S)

Ameerally, Niamatalli. Appan Jaat: a Play in One Act. [type-
script] (D)

Anderson, Megan. Change of Heart. [typescript] (D)

Anderson, Peter. [cf. Seymour, A.J.--"Greatness and Bitterness,"
and Pilgrim, Frank--So this is the Brink]

anonymous. "Comment," Kyk-Over-Al 26 (1959) p. 15 [on Wordsworth McAndrew's "Last Rites"] (E)

anonymous. "Drama in Guyana--Brief Survey," Kaie 3 (1966) p. 30 (E) anonymous. "Guiana's Welcome," Christmas Tide (1935) p. 60 (P)

anonymous. Midnight Musings in Demerara, or Poems on Various Subjects. London. 1832. (P)

anonymous. "Report on the Caribbean Writers and Artists Conference," Kaie 3 (1966) p. 3 (E)

anonymous. Stories from Guyana. Georgetown: Daily Chronicle, 1967. (S)

anonymous. Thoughts on British Guiana. By a Planter. 1847. (C)

Anthony, Compton. "I Swear," Chronicle Christmas Annual (1954) p. 19 (S)

Apata, Kwame. "Name Change," p. 37 Seymour's New Writing in the Caribbean (P)

_____. "Pan Man," p. 37 Seymour's New Writing in the Caribbean (P)

The Argosy. [Archives 1880-1907 incomplete] (X)

Armoogan, N. "Christmas Song," Chronicle Christmas Annual (1958) p. 35 (P)

Arno, William N. History of Victoria Village, E.C.D. Georgetown: Guyana Graphic, 1966. (C)

Ashton, W. The Syndicate Horse and Other Stories. Demerara, 1898. (S)

Athos. (pseud.) "The Yellow Flower," Chronicle Christmas Annual (1950) p. 40 (S)

Aunty Belinda. (pseud.) "Wha Happen Dis Year?" Christmas Tide (1923) p. 31 (C)

Azevedo, Hilda. "The Call," Christmas Tide (1936) p. 93 (S)

_____. "Hearts-Ease and Madonnas," Christmas Tide (1935) p. 71 (S)

B

B., D.F. "A Love Song to My Wife," p. 103 Cameron's Guianese Poetry... (P)

B., R.O. "A Father to His Child," Christmas Tide (1934) p. 6 (P)

B., W. Geoffrey. *Conversation p. 17/I Don't Really See People p. 16/A Dusty Dray Drawn... p. 18/Mangoes p. 15 Expression 3¹. (1967) (P)

Bacchus, Sam N. "A Desperate Deception," Chronicle Christmas Annual (1952) p. 13 (S)

Bajantoad. (pseud.?) "The Divorce House," <u>Christmas Tide</u> (1936)
    p. 84 (S)

Baldwin, R. "The Cigarette Packet," <u>Chronicle Christmas Annual</u>
    (1954) p. 23 (S)

_____. "The Watcher by the River," <u>Christmas Tide</u> (1950)
    p. 21 (S)

_____. "The Window," <u>Chronicle Christmas Annual</u> (1952) p. 42 (S)

Balgobin, Basil. <u>Asra. A Political Play of India</u>. perf.
    Guyana 1945 (D)

_____. "Box Money," <u>Chronicle Christmas Annual</u> (1952) p. 25 (S)

_____. "Common Ground," <u>Caribia</u> (1951/52) p. 31 (S)

_____. "The Cricket Match," <u>Christmas Tide</u> (1947) p. 6 (S)

_____. "The Di-Di's Tree," <u>Christmas Tide</u> (1948) p. 12 (S)

_____. "Eggs for Christmas," <u>Chronicle Christmas Annual</u>
    (1961) p. 19 (S)

_____. "The Goat Society," <u>Chronicle Christmas Annual</u> (1953)
    p. 17 (S)

_____. "Jungle Episode," <u>Caribia</u> (1949/50) p. 69 (S)

_____. "Medicine Man," <u>Kyk-Over-Al</u> 11 (1950) p. 48 (S)

_____. "The Parson's Tea," <u>Chronicle Christmas Annual</u> (1946)
    p. 5 (S)

_____. "Sammy Finds a Way," <u>Chronicle Christmas Annual</u> (1946)
    p. 40 (S)

_____. "This is My Country," <u>Christmas Tide</u> (1949) p. 13 (S)

Barclay, Carmen. "The Giant," <u>Chronicle Christmas Annual</u> (1967)
    p. 16 (P)

Barclay, Cynthia. "Drought Poem," <u>Expression I</u> (1966) p. 18 (P)

Barclay, Frederick. "Kill My Love," <u>Chronicle Christmas Annual</u>
    (1951) p. 9 (S)

Barclay, Leslie. "The Picture," <u>Christmas Tide</u> (1948) p. 6 (S)

Barrington-Brown, C. "Mount Roraima," p. 19 Seymour's <u>My Lovely
    Native Land</u> (T)

Barrow, Charles. "Delight," p. 24 R.C. McAndrew's <u>Plexus</u> (P)

_____. "In the Beginning," p. 24 R.C. McAndrew's <u>Plexus</u> (P)

_____. "Limit," <u>Poet</u> 13, 1 (1972) p. 3 also <u>Expression Six</u>
    (1960) p. 26 (P)

_____. "The New Girl," p. 16 R.C. McAndrew's <u>Plexus</u> (P)

_____. "Saturday," <u>Expression Six</u> (1960) p. 26 (P)

_____. "Somewhere Beside the Sea," p. 6 R.C. McAndrew's <u>Plexus</u> (P)

Barry, Vincent. "The Golden Ocelot," broadcast Radio Demerara
    1968 (S)

_____. "Melon," broadcast Radio Demerara 1968 (S)

Bartrum, Eugene. "Back Ground," Kyk-Over-Al 8 (1949) p. 13 (S)

_____. "Buried Treasures," Kyk-Over-Al 13 (1951) p. 231 (S)

_____. "Frills," Christmas Tide (1950) p. 8 (S)

_____. "Love Came Down..." Kyk-Over-Al 11 (1950) p. 17 (S)

_____. "Out of their Hearts," Chronicle Christmas Annual
    (1950) p. 6 (S)

_____. "Pretty Poll," Kyk-Over-Al 6 (1948) p. 26 (S)

_____. "Productive Dollars," Chronicle Christmas Annual (1948.
    p. 14 (S)

_____. "Red Light," Kyk-Over-Al 12 (1951) p. 100 (S)

_____. "Roses for Room 5," Caribia (1948/49) p. 29 (S)

_____. "So Deep is the Night," Chronicle Christmas Annual
    (1954) p. 12 (S)

_____. "Strange Catch," Christmas Tide (1948) p. 23 (S)

_____. "Tattered Soles," Christmas Tide (1949) p. 68 (S)

Bascom, N.J.A. "A Desperate Expedient," Christmas Tide (1921)
    p. 3 (S)

Baugh, Edward. West Indian Poetry 1900-1970. A Study in Cul-
    tural Decolonisation. Savacou Publication, Ltd. n.d. (Cr)

Bayley, Jack. (pseud.?) "Painless Extraction," Caribia (1946/47)
    p. 55 (S)

Bayley, Margaret Evelyn. *The Breach p. 18/The Tropics p. 36
    Elma Seymour's Sun is a Shapely Fire (P)

Beke, X. [pseud. cf. Hawtayne, G.H.]

Belgrave, Audrey. "Bamboo," Chronicle Christmas Annual (1949)
    p. 52 (S)

Belgrave, F.A. Poems. 1864. (P)

Benjamin, Colin. "After Thirteen Years," Chronicle Christmas
    Annual (1966) p. 15 (S)

Benjamin, Miriam. "To Innocent Posterity," Kaie 8 (1971) p. 32 (P

Benn, Denis Martin. Atta, Cuffy, and Accabre: An Historical
    Play in Verse in Four Acts. [typescript] (D)

_____. Pickpockets Anonymous. British Guiana, 1963. (D)

_____. Toussaint L'Ouverture; A Struggle for Freedom: An
    Historical Drama in Verse. 1968 [typescript] (D)

Berbice Gazette. [Archives 1813-1901 incomplete] (X)

erbice Gazette Penny Weekly. [Archives 1891-1892 incomplete] (X)

ernard, D.M.A. *Crescendo p. 24/Market Girl p. 12 Expression I
    (1966) (P)

_____. "Overheard," Expression 2 (1967) p. 20 (P)

ernard, David V. "The Future of British Guiana," Chronicle
    Christmas Annual (1949) p. 57 (P)

est, Alec. *The Falling Leaf p. 13/In the Cavern of My Blood
    p. 12/Lines on a Little Girl Drowned p. 12 Kyk-Over-Al 23
    (1958) (P)

_____. "Memorial Blues for Billie Holliday," New World
    (Fortnightly) I (1964) p. 9 (P)

_____. "Six Poems by Alec Best." *Ahmad Jamal p. 26/As Be-
    tween the Sea's Expansive Benevolence p. 24/If I Had the Power
    p. 25/If They Should Ask p. 21/The Nights p. 22/Scenery
    Searching for a Soul p. 23 New World (Fortnightly) 20 (1965)(P)

_____. "Wedding March for Daphne," Kyk-Over-Al 27 (1960)
    p. 67 (P)

hagwandai. "To a Water Lily," p. 68 Elma Seymour's Sun is a
    Shapely Fire (P)

hagwandin, Balwant. *Our Mirror p. 24/Parenthesis p. 10 R.C.
    McAndrew's Plexus (P)

_____. "The Valet," p. 16 R.C. McAndrew's Plexus (S)

hattacharya, Brojo. *Rice-Harvest p. 189/The 63 Beach p. 188/
    The Two Shores p. 187 Kyk-Over-Al 28 (1961) (P)

im. ed. Barbados by Frank A. Collymore from 1942--onwards.
    [cf. An Index to Bim] (J)

irbalsingh, F.M. "Edgar Mittelholzer: Moralist or Pornog-
    rapher?" Journal of Commonwealth Literature 7 (1969) p. 88 (E)

_____. "'Escapism' in the Novels of John Hearne," Caribbean
    Quarterly 16, 1 (1970) p. 28 (E)

_____. "The Novels of Ralph De Boissière," Journal of Common-
    wealth Literature 9 (1970) p. 104 (E)

_____. "To John Bull, with Hate," Caribbean Quarterly 14,4
    (1968) p. 74 [on E.R. Braithwaite's books] (E)

_____. "W. Adolphe Roberts: Creole Romantic," Caribbean
    Quarterly 19,2 (1973) p. 100 (E)

ishram, Kenneth. "A Christmas Masquerade," Chronicle Christmas
    Annual (1959) p. 61 (P)

lades, S.E. "Thanksgiving Hymn," p. 141 Cameron's Guianese
    Poetry... (P)

land, Muriel. "The Plaque," Chronicle Christmas Annual (1954)
    p. 5 (S)

Bobb, Cecily. "No Ovations," <u>Chronicle Christmas Annual</u> (1967) p. 21 (P)

Bolingbroke, H. <u>A Voyage to the Demerary, Containing a Statis-tical Account of the Settlements There and of Those of the Essequebo, the Berbice and other Rivers of Guyana ... 1799-1806.</u> Norwich, 1807. Philadelphia, 1813. (T,C)

_____. <u>A Voyage to the Demerary by Henry Bolingbroke 1799-1806.</u> Georgetown: Daily Chronicle, 1947. [Guyana Edition ed. Vincent Roth] (T,C)

<u>Booker News</u>. Georgetown. [Bookers employees newspaper] (X)

Boston, Cecil G. "Reunion," <u>Chronicle Christmas Annual</u> (1958) p. 4 (S)

Bourne, J.A.V. "Big Bear," <u>Chronicle Christmas Annual</u> (1945) p. 44 and <u>Kyk-Over-Al</u> 4 (1947) p. 32 (S)

_____. "Death in the Night," <u>Kyk-Over-Al</u> 3 (1946) p. 16 (S)

_____. <u>Dreams, Devils, Vampires: Short Stories</u>. Georgetown: F.A. Persick, 1940. *Dream Magic/The Thing of Evil/The Green Chest from Eldorado/Orange Blossoms and Tragedy/Bartica Inter-lude/The Death of a Vampire [Stories reprinted from <u>Chronicle Christmas Annual</u>] (S)

_____. "Guyana Rapture," <u>Chronicle Christmas Annual</u> (1951) p. 14 (S)

_____. "Last Day," <u>Kyk-Over-Al</u> 6 (1948) p. 46 (S)

_____. "Marionne," <u>Kyk-Over-Al</u> 1 (1945) p. 9 (P)

_____. "Miracles Do Not Happen," <u>Kyk-Over-Al</u> 1 (1945) p. 47 (S

_____. "Portrait of Mrs. Dolly," <u>Kyk-Over-Al</u> 3 (1946) p. 7 (P)

_____. "Tuesday!" <u>Kyk-Over-Al</u> 2 (1946) p. 24 (S)

Bourne, Tommy. <u>Hassa Curry: A Caribbean One Act Play</u>. British Guiana: Labour Advocate, 1958. (D)

_____. <u>Mackenzie Blues: A Play in One Act</u>. [typescript] (D)

Bourne, W.A. "The Image," <u>Chronicle Christmas Annual</u> (1945) p. 6 (S)

_____. "Thoughts," <u>Chronicle Christmas Annual</u> (1945) p. 46 (P)

Bowrey, S. "The Campanero or Bell-Bird," <u>Christmas Tide</u> (1935) p. 53 (P)

_____. "Digging Protected Treasure," <u>Christmas Tide</u> (1935) p. 41 (S)

Boxill, Anthony. "A Bibliography of West Indian Fiction," <u>World Literature Written in English</u> 19 (1971) p. 23 (Z)

Boyce, Duncan. "Water Money," <u>Kyk-Over-Al</u> 1 (1945) p. 22 (S)

Boyle, A. Chronic. (pseud.) "The Clue of the Crushed Canetop," Christmas Tide (1935) p. 26 (S)

Boyce, Winston. "Demerara," New World (Fortnightly) 34 (1966) p. 26 (S)

Braithwaite, Edward R. Choice of Straws. London: Bodley Head, 1965. New York: Pyramid, 1972. (N)

_____. "Funeral," p. 92 Ramchand's West Indian Narrative [Excerpt from To Sir With Love] (N-e)

_____. A Kind of Homecoming. Englewood Cliffs: Prentice Hall, 1962. London: Muller, 1963. (A)

_____. "Minutes of Grace," p. 199 Salkey's West Indian Stories (S)

_____. "The P.T. Class," p. 88 Ramchand's West Indian Narrative [Excerpt from To Sir With Love] (N-e)

_____. "The Pawpaw," p. 9 Walmsley's The Sun's Eye (P)

_____. Paid Servant. New York: McGraw-Hill, 1968; Pyramid, 1972 (A)

_____. Reluctant Neighbours. London: Bodley Head, 1972. New York: McGraw-Hill, 1972. (A)

_____. "Rites," p. 76 Thieme's Anthology of West Indian Literature (P)

_____. To Sir With Love. London: Bodley Head, 1959. Englewood Cliffs: Prentice-Hall, 1960, 1962. New York: Pyramid, 1973. (A)

Braithwaite, I.E. "Kyk-Over-Al and the Radicals," New World (1966) p. 55 [Guyana Independence Issue] (E)

_____. "Gold (For Wilson Harris)," Poet 13, 1 (1972) p. 3 (P)

Brathwaite, Percy A. (comp.) Folksongs of Guyana: Queh-Queh, Chanties and Ragtime. Georgetown: C.A. Welshman, 1964. (M)

_____. (comp.) and Serena Brathwaite (ed.) Guyanese Proverbs and Stories. Georgetown, 1966. (F)

_____. The Legend of Christmas: Stories and Verse. Georgetown: author, 1973. (S,P)

_____. Musical Traditions. Georgetown: C.A. Welshman, 1962. (Y)

Brassington, F.E. "Daybreak," Kyk-Over-Al 7 (1948) p. 3 and 19 (1954) p. 89 (P)

_____. Poems. Georgetown: Argosy Co., 1941. *Sincerity/Two Friends/Rain/Clouds/City Lights/Reminiscence/A Flight of Fancy/ Peace Thoughts, 1940/Requiescat/Frustration/Resurrection/The Power of Music/The Letter/Narcissus/The Ideal/In Sleep/I Wish/ The Soldier's Farewell/Jitterbug (P)

Brent, Peter Ludwig. (ed.) Young Commonwealth Poetry. London: Heinemann, 1965. (P)

Brett, (Rev.) William Henry. The Indian Tribes of Guiana: Their Condition and Habits. London: Bell and Daldy, 1868. (C,F)

_____. Legends and Myths of the Aboriginal Indians of British Guiana. London: William Wells Gardner, 1860, 1861. (F)

_____, and Leonard Lambert. (eds.) Guiana Legends. London: Society for the Propagation of the Gospel in Foreign Parts, 1931. (F)

British Guiana Courier. [Archives 1834 incomplete] (X)

Britton, Peter S. "Brenda's Pretence," Chronicle Christmas Annual (1955) p. 20 (S)

Brock, Ian. "The Monster Hoax," Chronicle Christmas Annual (1961) p. 35 (S)

The British Guiana Bulletin. [Fortnightly] (X)

Bronkhurst, H.V.P. Among the Hindus and Creoles of British Guyana. London: T. Woolmer, 1888. (C)

Bryant, W. Hawley. "Song of Guiana's Children," Kyk-Over-Al 19 (1954) p. 68 (P)

Bryce, Elma. [pseud. cf. Seymour, A.J.--"Christmas Gift"]

Burnham, Forbes. A Destiny to Mould. Selected Discourses by the Prime Minister of Guyana. London: Longman Caribbean, 1970. [comp. by C.A. Nascimento and R.A. Burrowes. Foreward by Martin Carter] (C)

Burrowes, Edward R. "A Christmas Hymn," Chronicle Christmas Annual (1958) p. 11 (S)

_____. "The Singing Ghost of Chateau Margot," Chronicle Christmas Annual (1960) p. 16 (S)

Burton, Garfield. "Prophecy (March 1952)," Kyk-Over-Al 15 (1952) p. 71 (P)

Butisingh, Randall. "Land Mark at Chateau Margot," Kaie 10 (1973) p. 22 (P)

_____. Love's Light. Georgetown: Advance Press, 1972. *O You Who Cannot See the Sun/Helen Keller (An Inspiration)/ Saint Francis of Assisi/I Do Not Ask to See Thy Face/My Heart Sings/My Neighbour/The Beggar/He Sang/Beggar of Song/Memories/ Handful of Coins/Love's Quest/Cheerful Day/Oasis of Delight/ Light Divine/I Ask for Nought (P)

_____. Poems from Annandale. Georgetown: Annandale Writers Group Publication, 1973. *He Sang/Landmark at Chateau Margot/ Wild Flowers/The Moon/The Saint [cf. also Persaud, Brahmdeo and Monar, M.R. Each of the three writers has five poems in the vol.] (P)

_____. "Raindrops," p. 10 Monar's <u>Poems for Guyanese Children</u> (P)

_____. <u>Wild Flowers and Other Poems</u>. Georgetown, 1972. *Vigilance Beach 1945/God's Image/Suppress Your Tear/Wild Flowers/Love-Light/Landmark at Chateau Margot/New-Blown Lilies/The Farmer/Raindrops/Life's Precious Gift/Yellow-Leaf/Love's Balm/The Dancer/Rain and Sun (P)

Butler, Vivian F. "The Plantation Trespasser," <u>Chronicle Christmas Annual</u> (1948) p. 12 (S)

Butt, Audrey J. "A Study of the System of Beliefs on the Carib-Speaking Akawaio of British Guiana," <u>Social and Economic Studies</u> 2, 1 (1953) p. 102 (C)

Buttrey, W.A. *Divine Love p. 168/The Happy Toiler p. 162/Mighty Mazaruni p. 74/Noble Thoughts and Noble Actions p. 149/The Owl p. 84/When Things Seem Dark p. 150/The Wonder Clock p. 132 Cameron's <u>Guianese Poetry...</u> (P)

_____. "The Traveller's Tale," <u>Christmas Tide</u> (1934) p. 17 (P)

Byass, Charles. "Just a Matter of Love," <u>Chronicle Christmas Annual</u> (1947) p. 27 (S)

Byass, Lawrence. "Miracle at Dusk," <u>Chronicle Christmas Annual</u> (1946) p. 6 (S)

_____. "The Old House," <u>Kyk-Over-Al</u> 12 (1951) p. 152 (S)

C

C., S. *And There Shall Be No More Sea p. 21/At the Crossings p. 6/The Bird p. 14/The Bumble Bee p. 6/Cheer p. 21/England p. 12/Hymn p. 17/The King p. 14/The Moon in Beauty Rose p. 21/Pretty Morning p. 14/Sunrise p. 12/That's That p. 6/Winnie p. 6 <u>Chronicle Christmas Annual</u> (1949) (P)

Calder, Aubrey. "Death Trap," Georgetown <u>Sunday Chronicle</u> (P)

_____. "The Limers Creed," Georgetown <u>Sunday Argosy</u> (P)

_____. "Those Magical Moments," Georgetown <u>Sunday Argosy</u> (P)

_____. "We Welcome You <u>Contact</u>," [in initial issue of <u>Contact</u>, a Caribbean region newspaper] (P)

Callender, H.T. "As Desired," <u>Christmas Tide</u> (1934) p. 18 (S)

Cameron, Norman E. <u>Adoniya: A Play in Three Acts</u>. British Guiana: F.A. Persick, 1953. perf. Georgetown: Queen's College 1943. also in Cameron's <u>Three Immortals</u>. (D)

_____. Adventures in the Field of Culture. Georgetown: Daily Chronicle, 1971. (A)

_____. "The African Prince," p. 135 Cameron's Guianese Poetry ... (P)

_____. "All is Fair in Love," p. 129 Cameron's Guianese Poetry... (P)

_____. Balthasar. Georgetown: Argosy Co., 1931. (D)

_____. "Band Day in the Botanic Gardens," Poet 13, 1 (1972) p. 4 (P)

_____. "A Brave Boy," p. 153 Cameron's Guianese Poetry... (P)

_____. "Building a Tradition in Drama," Kyk-Over-Al 25 (1959) p. 120 (E)

_____. "Cultural Life in Jamaica," Kyk-Over-Al 7 (1948) p. 9 (E)

_____. "Drama in British Guiana," Kyk-Over-Al 1 (1945) p. 38 (E)

_____. Ebedmelech: A Play in Three Acts. British Guiana: F.A. Persick, 1953. also in Cameron's Three Immortals (D)

_____. The Evolution of the Negro. Georgetown: Argosy Co., 1934. 2 vols. [first publ. 1929] (C)

_____. (ed.) Guianese Poetry (Covering the Hundred Year Period 1831-1931). British Guiana: Argosy Co., 1931. Nendeln: Kraus, 1970. (P)

_____. Guide to the Published Works of a Guyanese Author and Playwright. Guyana: Labour Advocate Job Printing, 1966. [annotated bibliography of Cameron's work] (Z)

_____. Guyanese Library and Its Impact. Georgetown, 1971. [publ. in serial form in Sunday Chronicle 2-25 May 1969] (Cr,Z)

_____. A History of the Queen's College of British Guiana. Georgetown, 1951. (C)

_____. Interlude: Original Poems. Georgetown: Argosy Co., 1944. *Three Cricketing Resorts/A Gala Day with the B.G.F.A./ Three Sea Wall Scenes/The Travellers' Palm/On National Debt/ Depression/At Xmas Time/Human Pleasures/Adoniya--an Idyll/The Two Kittens/All is Fair in Love/Von Hoogenheim/The Maroon/The African Prince/On Character Building/On Action and Co-Action/ When Fear Brings Worry/On Honesty/On Falsehood/On Favouritism/ A Lovable Girl/Modern Womanhood/A Brave Boy/Know the Higher Men/Ye that Labour/Night/A Life Well Lived/The Supreme Example/ Peace, My Hurrying Heart!/The Two Stranded Sailors/Married Romance/Dawn on Vlissengen Road/A Pleasant Surprise/Band Day in the Botanic Gardens (P)

_____. Jamaica Joe: A Play in Three Acts. British Guiana: De Souza's Printery, 1962. perf. Georgetown: Queen's College, 1946 (D)

_____. *Kayssa, or; Hear the Other Side: Programme and Text of Play*. British Guiana: Adana Printing Service, 1959. (D)

_____. "Looking Backwards in the Cultural Field," *Kaie* 1 (1965) p. 6 (E)

_____. "On Favouritism," p. 114 Cameron's *Guianese Poetry*... (P)

_____. *Poetry and Philosophy in Drama*. Georgetown: Labour Advocate Job Printing, 1973. (Cr)

_____. *The Price of Victory: A Play in Two Parts (Based on Nigerian Legend)*. British Guiana: Labour Advocate Job Printing Dept., 1965. (D)

_____. *Sabaco: A Play in Three Acts*. British Guiana: F.A. Persick, 1953. perf. 1948. also in Cameron's *Three Immortals* (D)

_____. *Thoughts on Life and Literature*. British Guiana: F.A. Persick, 1950. (C, Cr)

_____. *Three Immortals: A Collection of Three Plays*. Georgetown: F.A. Persick, 1953. *Adoniya/Sabaco/Ebedemelech (D)

_____. "The Traveller's Palm" p. 40 Seymour's *Themes of Song* also p. 68 Elma Seymour's *Sun is a Shapely Fire* also *Kyk-Over-Al* 19 (1954) p. 92 (P)

_____. *The Trumpet. A Play in Three Acts*. Georgetown: Daily Chronicle, 1969. (D)

_____. "Von Hoogenheim," *Kyk-Over-Al* 19 (1954) p. 65 (P)

_____. "Walter Mac A. Lawrence," *Kyk-Over-Al* 2 (1946) p. 17 (E)

Cameron, Patricia. *Casuarina p. 17/History p. 15/Many Mansions p. 20/Rain p. 18 Douglas' *Guyana Drums* (P)

Campbell, John. "Cane-Cutter," p. 6 Monar's *Poems for Guyanese Children* also *Poet* 13,1 (1972) p. 5 (P)

_____. *Come Back to Melda*. perf. Guyana 1963 (D)

_____. *Cuffy, the Brazen: One Act Play*. [in anthology: cf. below Campbell's *Writers in Uniform*] (D)

_____. *Dhanwattie: A Play in One Scene*. perf. Georgetown: Theatre Guild 1966. (D)

_____. *Don't Look Back: A Play in One Act*. 1963 [typescript] (D)

_____. "Dress Down," *Kaie* 10 (1973) p. 25 (P)

_____. "Me Rights," *Poet* 13,1 (1972) p. 5 also p. 5 Trotman's *Voices of Guyana* (P)

_____. "Nigger Yard Woman" *Kaie* 10 (1973) p. 18 (P)

_____. *Our Own Poems*. Georgetown: Author, 1973. *The Lighthouse/What's for Dinner/John's Little Turkey/Let's Co-operate/

Kaieteur/My Relatives/The Zoo/The Residence/Linden Town/The
Bus from Rosignol/The District Policeman/Betsy Jane/The Hunter/
A Good Turn/The Little Boy from Sand Creek/Buxton Spice/Our
House/Guyana Products/The Dirty Pool/Quebana Boy/Orinduik/The
Things They Like/Tom Boy/Gabby Haynes/The Drink Men (P)

_____. Poems for All. Goergetown: Master Printery, 1971.
*Kaieteur/Cabbage Palms/My Cinderella/Life/Passive Poverty/
The Cane-Cutter/Me Rights/Up to Kumeran/Diamonds/Failure/The
Barriers/Dead Heroes/My Fall Brothers/God Made it So/Loyalty/
The Path/South Side People/Thoughts of an American Hippie/
Ophelia/Him/The Village Rape/The Old Baker's Shop/Wismar
Crossing/Crabman/The Old Canje Bridge/Our House/Retirement (P)

_____. Poems to Remember. Georgetown: Sheik M. Sadeek, 1968.
*Imagination/Wenamu/A Moment/Reflection/A Thought/The Blind
Girl/Truth/Up-River Scape/The Slave/The Cane Cutter (P)

_____. Trends 12. Georgetown: Labour Advocate Job Printing,
1973. *Trends/Change/Two Poets Muse/'Guana Dog/Dress Down/
Shark/The Sweet Whore/Nigger Yard Woman/Eye Pass/Guybau Awee
Own/Arise/The Gathering (P)

_____. "Wenamu," Kaie 5 (1968) p. 21 (P)

_____. (ed.) Writers in Uniform. Guyana: Guyana Police
Force Publication, 1972. [1 play, 2 stories, 13 poems by
Policemen] (Y)

Campbell, Owen. "Noretta," Kyk-Over-Al 12 (1951) p. 127 (P)

_____. "Prospect," Kyk-Over-Al 15 (1952) p. 73 (P)

_____. "Tourist," Kyk-Over-Al 12 (1951) p. 126 (P)

_____. "Ubi Gentium," Kyk-Over-Al 13 (1951) p. 228 (P)

_____. "The Vessels," Kyk-Over-Al 15 (1952) p. 72 (P)

Cappell, Evelyn. "Thousand Dollar Bill," Christmas Tide (1948)
p. 26 (S)

Carew, Jan [Carew, Ian Alwyn]. "Alone," p. 85 Figueroa's Caribbean Voices (P)

_____. "An Artist in Exile-from the West Indies," New World
(Fortnightly) 27/28 (1965) p. 23 (E)

_____. Anancy and Tiger: A Radio Play. broadcast B.B.C.,
196-? (D)

_____. Atta: A Radio Play. broadcast B.B.C., 196-? (D)

_____. "Barakara," p. 15 Seymour's My Lovely Native Land
also p. 21 Seymour's Themes of Song also Kyk-Over-Al 19
(1954) p. 77 (P)

_____. The Baron of South Boulevard: A One Hour Television
Play. televised B.B.C. 1963 (D)

_____. Behind God's Back: A Play for Television._ televised C.B.C. (Canada) 1969 (D)

_____. _The Big Pride._ televised A.T.V. (London) 1962 broadcast also as _University of Hunger_ (D)

_____. _Black Horse, White Rider: A Stage Play._ perf. at Venice Festival (Canada) 1969 (D)

_____. _Black Midas._ London: Secker and Warburg, 1958. [publ. also as _A Touch of Midas_] (N)

_____. "Black Midas," p. 17 Dathorne's _Caribbean Narrative_ also _New World_ (1966) p. 105 [Guyana Independence Issue] also p. 182 Ramchand's _West Indian Narrative_ (N-e)

_____. "Black Studies Seek Universal Goals," Georgetown _Sunday Chronicle_ (29 Dec. 1974) p. 7 (E)

_____. "Chaotic Epic," p. 16 Figueroa's _Caribbean Voices_ (P)

_____. "The Cities," _Kyk-Over-Al_ 12 (1951) p. 106 also _Kyk-Over-Al_ 19 (1954) p. 129 (P)

_____. "The Coming of Amalivaca," p. 125 Salkey's _West Indian Stories_ (F)

_____. _The Conversion of Tiho: A One Hour Television Play._ televised B.B.C. 1963 (D)

_____. _The Day of the Fox: A Play in Three Acts Adapted for Television._ televised B.B.C. 1962 (D)

_____. "The Dyke," _New World_ (Fortnightly) 23 (1965) p. 22 (P)

_____. _Exile from the Sun._ [typescript] (D)

_____. "The Eye," p. 15 Salkey's _Breaklight_ (P)

_____. _Gentlemen, Be Seated._ perf. Toronto Workshop 1967; Guyana 1968 (D)

_____. _Green Winter, A Novel._ New York: Stein & Day, 1965. [publ. also as _Moscow is Not My Mecca_] (N)

_____. "The Hostel," _Pepperpot_ 2,1 (1964) p. 60 (E)

_____. "Hunters and Hunted," p. 189 Salkey's _Stories from the Caribbean_ (S)

_____. "A Job with the Road Gang," p. 85 Walmsley's _The Sun's Eye_ [excerpt from _Black Midas_] (N-e)

_____. _The Last Barbarian._ London: Secker and Warburg, 1961.(N)

_____. _Legend of the Nameless Mountain: A Radio Play._ broadcast B.B.C. 1958; Jamaica 1960 (D)

_____. "Literature and Language in Developing Countries," _New World_ (Fortnightly) Part I= 22 (1965) p. 25. Part II= 23 (1965) p. 23 (E)

_____. "Love," New World (Fortnightly) 23 (1965) p. 22 (P)

_____. "Manarabisi," Kyk-Over-Al 19 (1954) p. 76 (P)

_____. Moscow is Not My Mecca. London: Secker and Warburg, 1964. [publ. also as Green Winter, A Novel] (N)

_____. No Gown for Peter: A One Hour Television Play. televised B.B.C. 1963 (D)

_____. Rape the Sun. New York: Third Press, 1973. (N)

_____. "The Reckoning," p. 68 Salkey's Caribbean Prose [excerpt from Black Midas] (N-e)

_____. "Requiem for my Sister," Kaie 4 (1967) p. 67 also New World (Fortnightly) 5 (1965) p. 45 (P)

_____. The Riverman. broadcast B.B.C. 1968, 1969; Jamaica 1960 (D)

_____. A Roof of Stars: A One Hour Television Play. 1963 [typescript] (D)

_____. The Smugglers: A One Hour Television Play. televised B.B.C. 1963 (D)

_____. "Some Aspects of Literature and Language in Developing Countries," AAW 2, 5 (1970) p. 190 (E)

_____. Streets of Eternity. British Guiana, 1952. *Atta/ The Reapers/Barakara/Manarabisi/Charcoal Burner (P)

_____. "Streets of Eternity. Atta." Kyk-Over-Al 15 (1952) P. 67 (P)

_____. "Ten Years," p. 51 Seymour's New Writing in the Caribbean also p. 189 Salkey's Breaklight [as "Ten Years: 1959-1969"] (P)

_____. "Tilson Ezekiel--Alias Ti-Zek," Georgetown Daily Chronicle (25 Dec. 1974) p. 22 (S)

_____. "Torment," Kyk-Over-Al 12 (1951) p. 171 (P)

_____. A Touch of Midas. New York: Coward, 1958. [publ. also as Black Midas] (N)

_____. "Toussaint l'Ouverture: A Reverie," New World (Fortnightly) 26 (1965) p. 3 also p. 11 Salkey's Breaklight (P)

_____. "Trespass," Kyk-Over-Al 15 (1952) p. 60 [excerpt from mss. Rivers of His Night] (N-e)

_____. "When I Returned," New World Quarterly 4,3 (1968) p. 55 also Poet 13,1 (1972) p. 6 (P)

_____. The Wild Coast. London: Secker and Warburg, 1958. (N)

_____. "The Wild Coast," p. 26 Dathorne's Caribbean Narrative (N-e)

_____. Winter in Moscow. New York: Avon, 1967. [adapted from his Green Winter which is same as Moscow is Not My Mecca] (N)

_____ and Sylvia Wynter. The University of Hunger. perf. Georgetown: Theatre Guild 1966 also broadcast B.B.C. 1961 [televised B.B.C. 1962 under title The Big Pride] (D)

Caribbean Authors. Georgetown: Public Free Library, 1972. [list of authors, dates of birth, language, nationality; does not include titles of their publications] (Z)

Caribbean Quarterly. Dept. of Extra-Mural Studies, U.W.I. Jamaica. [began 1949] (J)

Caribbean Quarterly: An Anthology of West Indian Poetry 5, 3 (1958) [pp. 121-226] (P)

Caribbean Studies. Univ. of Puerto Rico, Rio Piedras, P.R. [began 1961; each issue has "Current Bibliography" of West Indies] (J,Z)

Caribia (The Magazine of British Guiana and the West Indies). Georgetown, British Guiana [annual] (J)

Carless, Catherine. "Gypsy's Warning," Chronicle Christmas Annual (1950) p. 34 (S)

_____. "I Love You, Mr. Brown," Chronicle Christmas Annual (1949) p. 58 (S)

Carr, Alwyn R. *Awake the Flame/How Shall It End/Ode to Truth/Rapture Lab Talk. n.d. (P)

_____. *The Demon of Death/Demons of the Deep Lab Talk N.D. (S)

_____. *Native Song/Ode to a Martyr/The Seeds We Sow/The Receding Goal/A Drunk's Lament/Snake Cult/The Rain Storm/Labaria/Soul of the Universe/Thoughts for Christmas/Reflections on Time/Superstition/The Voice Within Lab Talk (July 1971) (P)

_____. "Weird Destiny," Chronicle Christmas Annual (1956) p. 18 (S)

Carr, Ernest A. et al. (eds.) Caribbean Anthology of Short Stories. Kingston: Pioneer Press, 1953. (S)

Carr, W.I. "Literature and Society," Caribbean Quarterly 8,2 (1962) p. 76 [based on open lecture at U.W.I., Jamaica 26 Nov. 1961] (E)

_____. "Reflections on the Novel in the British Caribbean," Queen's Quarterly 70,4 (1963/64) p. 585 (E)

_____. "Roger Mais--Design from a Legend," Caribbean Quarterly 13,1 (1967) p. 3 (E)

_____. "The West Indian Novelist: Prelude and Context," Caribbean Quarterly 11,1 and 2 (1965) p. 71 (E)

Carter, Martin. "After One Year," New World (Fortnightly) 1,2 (1964) p. 7 [cf. below: "Jail Me Quickly"] (P)

_____. "Anonymous," New World (Fortnightly) (1965) p. 24 (P)

_____. "Apart from Both," GISRA 5,4 (1974) p. 45 [culture and the artist in Guyana] (E)

_____. "A Banner for the Revolution," p. 91 Seymour's My Lovely Native Land (P)

_____. "Black Friday 1962," New World (Fortnightly) 1,2 (1964) [cf. below: "Jail Me Quickly"] (P)

_____. "Cartman of Dayclean," Poet 13,1 (1972) p. 7 also Kaie 1 (1965) p. 14 also p. 165 Salkey's Breaklight (P)

_____. "Childhood of a Voice," New World (Fortnightly) 4 (1964) p. 35 [cf. below: "Jail Me Quickly"] (P)

_____. "Conversations," Kyk-Over-Al 28 (1961) p. 154 also Poet 13,1 (1972) p. 8 also Kaie 1 (1965) p. 15 [7 poems] (P)

_____. "Cuyuni," p. 56 Seymour's New Writing in the Caribbean (P)

_____. "Death of a Comrade," p. 163 Salkey's Breaklight also p. 65 Ramchand and Gray's West Indian Poetry (P)

_____. "Death of a Slave," Kyk-Over-Al 14 (1952) p. 53 and 22 (1957) p. 11 also Kaie 4 (1967) p. 70 also p. 36 Ramchand and Gray's West Indian Poetry also p. 201 Livingston's Caribbean Rhythms (P)

_____. "Death of a Slave" [dance interpretation perf. Georgetown: Theatre Guild in Miss Phoebe] (P)

_____. "Ever With Me," GISRA 5,4 (1974) p. 64 (P)

_____. "For My Son," p. 45 Seymour's Themes of Song also p. 65 Seymour's My Lovely Native Land (P)

_____. "Fragment of Memory," p. 102 Searwar's Co-Operative Republic also p. 5 Forde's Talk of the Tamarinds (P)

_____. "A Guyanese Poet in Cardiff," Kaie 2 (1966) p. 18 [A.J. Seymour's interview of Carter after his participation in the Commonwealth Arts Festival in England] (I)

_____. The Hidden Man. Georgetown, 1952. *I Stretch My Hand/Cartman of Dayclean/Sunday Night/Looking Again/I Walk and Walk/Till I Collect/No Madness Like This Sanity (P)

_____. The Hill of Fire Glows Red. British Guiana: Master Printer, 1951. [Miniature Poet Series] *Not I With This Torn Shirt/Do Not Stare at Me/Old Higue/Like the Blood of Quamina/Shines the Beauty of My Darling/Three Years After This/Looking at Your Hands/Tomorrow and the World/It is for This That I am Furious/Run Shouting Through the Town/Listening to the Land/A Banner for the Revolution (P)

_____. "I Clench My Fist," p. 166 Salkey's Breaklight (P)

_____. "I Come from the Nigger Yard," p. 96 Salkey's Breaklight also p. 99 Searwar's Co-Operative Republic also p. 203 Livingston's Caribbean Rhythms also p. 5 A New Guyana (P)

_____. "If It Were Given," p. 57 Seymour's New Writing in the Caribbean (P)

_____. "Jail Me Quickly," New World (Fortnightly) 34 (1966) p. 21 *Black Friday 1962/After One Year/What Can a Man Do More/Where are Free Men/Childhood of a Voice (P)

_____. Kind Eagle. British Guiana, 1952. *Bare Night Without Comfort/Who Walks a Pavement/You Are Involved/O Where to Hide/The Kind Eagle/All of a Man/O Human Guide (P)

_____. "The Knife of Dawn," p. 84 Ramchand and Gray's West Indian Poetry (P)

_____. "The Leaves of Canna Lily," p. 57 Seymour's New Writing in the Caribbean (P)

_____. "A Letter," New World (Fortnightly) 1 (1964) p. 2 (C)

_____. "Listening to the Land," p. 14 Seymour's Themes of Song also p. 7 Seymour's My Lovely Native Land also p. 30 Forde's Talk of the Tamarinds also p. 43 Elma Seymour's Sun is a Shapely Fire (P)

_____. "Looking at Your Hands," Kyk-Over-Al 14 (1952) p. 52 also p. 102 Figueroa's Caribbean Voices also p. 66 Forde's Talk of the Tamarinds also p. 134 Salkey's Breaklight also p. 64 Seymour's My Lovely Native Land (P)

_____. Man and Making--Victim and Vehicle. Georgetown: National History and Arts Council, 1971. [text of 1971 Edgar Mittelholzer Memorial Lectures] (E)

_____. "New Day," Kyk-Over-Al 12 (1951) p. 114 (P)

_____. "Nigger Yard," New World Quarterly 3 (1963) p. 11 (P)

_____. "Not Hands Like Mine," p. 6 Trotman's Voices (P)

_____. "Occasion," p. 58 Thieme's Anthology of West Indian Literature also Savacou 3/4 (1970/71) p. 171 also p. 207 Livingston's Caribbean Rhythms (P)

_____. "Ode to Midnight," Kyk-Over-Al 6 (1948) p. 5 (P)

_____. "Old Higue," p. 13 Seymour's Fourteen Guianese Poems for Children (P)

_____. "On the Fourth Night of the Hunger Strike," p. 167 Salkey's Breaklight (P)

_____. "Out Out the Fire," Kyk-Over-Al 23 (1958) p. 37 (S)

_____. "Poem" [Someone, somewhere, shall know one day] New World (Fortnightly) 39 (1966) p. 2 (P)

19

_____. "Poem" [Strong memory, bright pressure of a hand] New World (Fortnightly) 19 (1965) p. 2 (P)

_____. "Poem" [What now we want to go with thunder] GISRA 4,3 (1973) p. 31 (P)

_____. "Poems of Prison," Kyk-Over-Al 15 (1952) p. 27 *Bare Night Without Comfort/Who Walks a Pavement/You Are Involved/ O Where to Hide/The Kind Eagle/All of a Man/O Human Guide/ The Discovery of Companion (P)

_____. Poems of Resistance from British Guiana. London: Lawrence and Wishart, 1954. *University of Hunger/I Am No Soldier/Death of a Slave/Death of a Comrade/Not Hands Like Mine/Letter 1/Letter 2/Letter 3/On the Fourth Night of the Hunger Strike/The Knife of Dawn/This is the Dark Time My Love/ You Are Involved/Weroon Weroon/I Come from the Nigger Yard/ Let Freedom Wake Him/Till I Collect/Cartman of Dayclean/I Clench My Fist (P)

_____. Poems of Resistance. Georgetown: University of Guyana 1964. [same contents as previous entry, with one addition: "A Banner for the Revolution"] (P)

_____. "Poems of Shape and Motion (I and II)," p. 204 Living- ston's Caribbean Rhythms [cf. below: "Three Poems of Shape and Motion--A Sequence"] (P)

_____. "Statement on Republic of Guyana," broadcast George- town (1 Aug. 1969) also publ. in booklet form by Guyana Ministry of Information (E)

_____. "There is No Riot," Georgetown Sunday Chronicle (23 Mar. 1975) p. 14 (P)

_____. "This is the Dark Time, My Love," p. 16 Salkey's Breaklight also p. 37 Ramchand and Gray's West Indian Poetry also p. 38 Thieme's Anthology of West Indian Literature also p. 46 Walmsley's The Sun's Eye (P)

_____. "Three Poems of Shape and Motion--A Sequence," Kyk- Over-Al 20 (1955) p. 141 (P)

_____. "Till I Collect," p. 38 Ramchand and Gray's West Indian Poetry (P)

_____. To A Dead Slave. British Guiana, 1951. (P)

_____. "Tomorrow and the World," p. 18 Seymour's Fourteen Guianese Poems for Children also p. 102 Seymour's My Lovely Native Land also p. 46 Seymour's Themes of Song (P)

_____. "Two Fragments of 'Returning'," Kyk-Over-Al 16 (1953) p. 138 (P)

_____. "University of Hunger," Kyk-Over-Al 14 (1952) p. 13 and 17 (1953) p. 208 and 22 (1957) p. 13 also Kaie 4 (1967) p. 71 also New World Quarterly 3 (1963) p. 56 also p. 23 Dathorne's Caribbean Verse (P)

_____. "Voices," Kyk-Over-Al 14 (1952) p. 12 and 22 (1957) p. 12 also The Tamarack Review 14 (1960) p. 58 also p. 133 Salkey's Breaklight (P)

_____. "We Walk the Streets," GISRA 5,4 (1974) p. 64 (P)

_____. "Weroon Weroon," New World Quarterly 3 (1963) p. 23 also p. 7 Monar's Poems for Guyanese Children (P)

_____. "What Can a Man Do More," New World (Fortnightly) 3 (1964) p. 7 [cf. above: "Jail Me Quickly"] (P)

_____. "Where Are Free Men," New World (Fortnightly) 4 (1964) p. 34 [cf. above: "Jail Me Quickly"] (P)

_____. "Words," Kyk-Over-Al 14 (1952) p. 13 and 22 (1957) p. 13 also The Tamarack Review 14 (1960) p. 47 (P)

_____. "You Are Involved," New World Quarterly 3 (1963) p. 72 also Poet 13, 1 (1972) p. 8 also p. 135 Salkey's Breaklight also p. 203 Livingston's Caribbean Rhythms (P)

_____. [cf. Seymour, A.J.--"The Arts in Guiana"]

_____. [cf. Seymour, A.J.--"Greatness and Bitterness"]

_____. [cf. Seymour, A.J.--"Is There a West Indian Way of Life?"]

Cartey, William. "The Rhythm of Society and Landscape: Mittelholzer, Carew, Williams, Dathorne," New World [Guyana Independence Issue] (1966) p. 96 (E)

Casson, (Rev.) M.A. "A New Year's Advice," Christmas Tide (1923) p. 26 (P)

Catholic Standard. [weekly newspaper of Georgetown Diocese] (X)

Cavigholi, Florence. "Lulu an the Camoodi," Kyk-Over-Al 26 (1959) p. 41 (F)

Cendrecourt, C. Julian. "Dreams," Christmas Tide (1938) p. 17 (P)

Cendrecourt, Esme. Captain's Party: A Play. New York, 19-? (D)

_____. Grandpapa's Pride: A Play in Three Acts. British Guiana, 1933. perf. Georgetown, 1942 [typescript] (D)

_____. New Probationer: A Play in Three Acts. British Guiana, 1939 [typescript] (D)

_____. Night in the Caribbean: A Play. New York, 19-? [typescript] (D)

_____. Romance of the Kaiteur: A Play in Three Acts. British Guiana, 1931. [typescript] (D)

_____. Unmasked: A Play in Three Acts. British Guiana, 1944 [typescript] (D)

Chabrol, Monica. "Dawn," Christmas Tide (1956) p. 12 (P)

Chamberlin, David. Smith of Demerara. London: Colonial Missionary Society, 1923. (B)

Chan, Brian. *About Him p. 26/Benediction p. 26/Grope p. 28/On
the Beach p. 27/A Purer Sense p. 26/A Slight Rose p. 25/To
Signify Something p. 27 Expression 4 (1968) (P)

_____. *The Ant p. 11/An Autobiography p. 10/Human Rights p.
9/Poem at Noon in Georgetown p. 10/The Reminder p. 9/You're
Quiet Tonight p. 12 Expression Six (1970) (P)

_____. *The Conditions of Balance p. 24/The New Man p. 21/
Nowadays p. 23/Old Lady p. 21/She Wears...p. 26/Walking Down
p. 25 Expression 3½ (1967) (P)

_____. *Fragments p. 18/I Wouldn't Like p. 14/My Brother's
Ghost p. 15/The Old Men p. 16 Expression 2 (1967) (P)

_____. *If I Could Extract p. 17/Which is Our Concern p. 11/
Youth Has Nothing to Say p. 5 Expression I (1966) (P)

_____. "Part One," Expression Six (1970) p. 27 (S)

_____. "Which is Our Concern," Poet 13,1 (1972) p. 8 (P)

_____. [cf. Drepaul, Michael -- Expression 4]

Chan, Royden V. "Memories," Chronicle Christmas Annual (1958)
p. 16 (S)

Chan-a-Sue, Derek. "August," Chronicle Christmas Annual (1967)
p. 75 also Expression 3½ (1967) p. 35 also Poet 13,1 (1972)
p. 9 (P)

_____. "Ode to a Guitar," Expression I (1966) p. 16 (P)

_____. "The Solitary Hut," Expression 2 (1967) p. 21 (P)

Chancellor, Bertie W. "It Makes You Think," broadcast Radio
Demerara 1968 (S)

_____. 26 Tiger Bay Alley: or, the Lord Will Provide: A Play
for Radio in One Act. [typescript] (D)

Chandisingh, Ralph E. "The Gown," Chronicle Christmas Annual
(1952) p. 18 (S)

_____. "Lenore," Chronicle Christmas Annual (1956) p. 24 (S)

_____. "The Singer," Chronicle Christmas Annual (1953)
P. 14 (S)

_____. "A Song of Farewell," Kyk-Over-Al 18 (1954) p. 23 (P)

_____. "Wings for an Angel," Christmas Tide (1956) p. 19 (S)

Chapman. "Epic Poem on Guiana," Timehri 12 [New Series 7,1]
(June 1893) (P)

Charles, Bertram. The Alexin of Our Cure. Georgetown: Author,
1970. (D)

_____. Another Man: Play in Two Acts. perf. Guyana 1968 (D)

_____. Another Place, Somewhere: Play in Two Acts. perf. Guyana 1969 (D)

_____. The End of the Affair. Georgetown, 1968. (D)

_____. The Human Predicament. broadcast Guyana Broadcasting Service 1971 (D)

_____. It Tolls Not for Thee: Play in One Act. perf. Guyana 1970 (D)

_____. The Lost Husband: Play in One Act. perf. Guyana 1970 (D)

_____. Our Dilemma. Georgetown: Author, 1972. *A Meal in the Moonlight/Our Dilemma/Only at Harvest Time/The Portuguese Bread-Seller/The Mud on the Walls/Tomorrow's Dinner/The Evil Spirits/Tony and Grumble/The Wedding/The Woman and the House/ A Touch of Tenderness/Another Time/A Friend/June Powell/A Woman With a Purpose/The Hypocrite/Only the Outside/The Woman on the Wind/The Idol/The Pick-Pocket (S)

_____. The Pains of Abortion: Play in One Act. Guyana, 1967 (D)

_____. A Virgin Child: Play in Two Acts. perf. Guyana 1967 (D)

_____. Within Our Narrow Walls: Play in Five Acts. perf. Guyana 1971 (D)

Charles, C.A. "The Sea is Free," Caribia (1951/52) p. 21 (S)

Chase, L.R. "Cultural Memories," Kyk-Over-Al 2 (1946) p. 31 (E)

Chase, Sam. The Collapsible Bridegroom (D)

_____. The Dreamer and the Jar (D)

_____. Gentlemen, the King (D)

_____. Guardroom Jitters (D)

_____. The Mare and the Bonds (D)

_____. The Ruler and the Boo-Boo Man (D)

Chase, Stella M. *Guiana the Beautiful p. 73/Sweet Contentment p. 37 Chronicle Christmas Annual (1957) (P)

_____. *Ode to Nature p. 34/The Stream p. 29 Chronicle Christmas Annual (1958) (P)

Chattoram, Paul. "The Best Man in the Village," Caribia (1954) (S)

_____. The Fall of an Idol. perf. Guyana 1970 (D)

_____. "The Key to a Quiet Holiday," Kaie 6 (1970) p. 9 (S)

_____. "The Last Run," Kaie 8 (1971) p. 66 [publ. under pseud. Walter O. Smith] (S)

Chattoram, Puran. <u>A Bridle for the Tongue: A Sketch</u>. British
Guiana, 19-? perf. Georgetown: Inter-School Drama Festival
1964 (D)

_____. <u>Vote for Me: A Play for Radio in One Act</u>. British
Guiana 19-? [typescript] (D)

Chinapen, Jacob Wellien. "Albion Wilds," <u>Kyk-Over-Al</u> 19 (1954)
p. 74 also p. 14 Ramcharitar-Lalla's <u>Anthology of Local
Indian Verse</u> (P)

_____. <u>Albion Wilds</u>. British Guiana: B.G. Lithographic Co.,
1961. *Albion Wilds/I Know a Bower/Strewn Petals/Invitation/
The Prisoner's Song/In Nature's Lap/Simple Charms/A Prayer/
Bright-Eyed Maiden/In a Garden/To a Humming-Bird/The Wren/
To a Flower (The Carrion-Crow Bush)/Day's Symphony/O Woman,
What Are You?/Crossing the Berbice/To a Flamboyant/The Flute
Divine/Columbus/At Eve/Glimpses of Immortality/On the Beach at
No. 63/I/To Veka (On His Seventh Birthday)/A Reverie/Guyana!
Loved Guyana! (P)

_____. "Crossing the Berbice One Evening," p. 20 Seymour's
<u>Themes of Song</u> also p. 16 Elma Seymour's <u>Sun is a Shapely
Fire</u> (P)

_____. "The Flute Divine," Gora Singh's <u>Heritage</u> (P)

_____. "Guyana! Loved Guyana!" p. 64 <u>A New Guyana</u> also
p. 12 Seymour's <u>Themes of Song</u> (P)

_____. "In the Fields," p. 38 Ramcharitar-Lalla's <u>Anthology
of Local Indian Verse</u> (P)

_____. "On the Beach at 63," p. 19 Seymour's <u>Themes of
Song</u> (P)

_____. "Peter Ruhoman," <u>Kaie</u> 2 (1966) p. 59 (B,Cr)

_____. "To Love," p. 44 Ramcharitar-Lalla's <u>Anthology of
Local Indian Verse</u> (P)

_____. "To the Flambouyant," p. 41 Seymour's <u>Themes of Song</u>
also p. 64 Elma Seymour's <u>Sun is a Shapely Fire</u> (P)

Cholmondeley, H.M.E. [cf. Seymour, A.J.--"Is There a West Indian
Way of Life?"]

<u>Christmas Tide--The Colony's Annual</u>. Georgetown: The Argosy Co.
[1st issue of this annual appeared 1893; irregular: by 1956,
only 49 <u>Christmas Tide</u> issues had been published; some issues
between 1921 and 1956 available in Georgetown] (J)

Christiani, Joan.(comp.) <u>A.J. Seymour. A Bibliography</u>.
Georgetown: National Library, 1974. [comprehensive] (Z)

<u>The Chronicle Christmas Annual</u>. Georgetown: Daily Chronicle,
Ltd. [began publ. 1916? irregular: copies 1945-1967 avail.
in Georgetown libraries, except 1962-1965 when no annuals
publ.] (J)

Chronicle Senanal. [Archives 1897-1899 incomplete] (X)

Chung, Geoffrey R. <u>Cottage Hospital: A Play in the Vernacular in Four Scenes.</u> [typescript] (D)

The Church and Colony. [Archives 1893 incomplete] (X)

Clarke, Preston. "We Waited for the Dawn," <u>Kyk-Over-Al</u> 19 (1954) p. 87 (P)

Clementi, (Sir) Cecil. <u>The Chinese in British Guiana.</u> Georgetown: Argosy Co., 1915. (B,C)

_____. "Kaietuk," <u>Timehri</u> 26 (1944) p. 60   also <u>Kyk-Over-Al</u> 19 (1954) p. 78 (P)

_____. "Roraima," <u>Timehri</u> 26 (1944) p. 60 also <u>Kyk-Over-Al</u> 19 (1954) p. 76 also p. 22 Seymour's <u>My Lovely Native Land</u> also p. 20 Seymour's <u>Themes of Song</u> (P)

Collier, Dorothy. <u>Five Plays.</u> Georgetown: Daily Chronicle, 1948. *Marry in Haste/Love is Blind/Plain Sailing/Married-- Yet Happy/Quiverful (D)

Collins, Bertram Aggrey Nathaniel. "Dark River," <u>Caribia</u> (1947/ 48) p. 44 (S)

_____. "Signs of the Times," <u>Chronicle Christmas Annual</u> (1947) p. 41 (P)

Colonist, 1832. (pseud.) *Beauty p. 61/Stanzas on the Waters p. 70/Song to a Sleeping Maiden p. 101/The Meeting p. 102/ Triumphal Return of a Victorious Army p. 110/A Wish p. 152/ Sudden Death p. 165/Death of Carl Friedrich Ernest von Weber, Composer p. 166 Cameron's <u>Guianese Poetry...</u> (P)

The Colonist. [Archives 1848-1884 incomplete] (X)

Comitas, Lambros. <u>Caribbeana 1900-1965. A Topical Bibliography.</u> Seattle: Univ. of Washington Press, 1968. [includes Guyana] (Z)

Cooksey, C. "Warao Stories," <u>Timehri</u> 7 [third series] (1921) p. 90 (F)

Cornette, E. Edwin. "Beaten by Science," <u>Christmas Tide</u> (1936) p. 34 (S)

_____. "The Neglected Country," <u>Christmas Tide</u> (1936) p. 27 (P)

Correia, Juliett. "Dedicated to the National Service Marchers," Georgetown <u>Sunday Chronicle</u> (16 Mar. 1975) p. 25 (P)

Corsbie, Ken. <u>My Name is Slave.</u> perf. Georgetown Theatre Guild 1970 also broadcast Guyana Broadcasting Service 1970 (D)

Cosson, Mortimer A. "Come Raise Your Voices," <u>Kyk-Over-Al</u> 19 (1954) p. 131 (P)

_____. "My Native Land," p. 43 <u>A New Guyana</u> (P)

Cotton, Brian. "Streets," <u>New World</u> (Fortnightly) 43 (1966) p. 24 (P)

_____ and N.D. Williams.(eds.) Expression I. Georgetown: the editors, 1966. [cf. below: Expression] (P)

Cotton, Cob. [pseud. cf. Gomes, Clement A.]

Craig, Dennis, "Age," Savacou 3/4 (1970/71) p. 142 (P)

_____. "The Day the Nation Mourned," p. 39 Figueroa's Caribbean Voices (P)

_____. "Flowers," p. 38 Donald Wilson's New Ships (P)

_____. "Interlude for Native Pride," p. 172 Figueroa's Caribbean Voices (P)

_____. "Lord of the Strange," Chronicle Christmas Annual (1947) p. 22 (S)

_____. "Pharoah Wept," Chronicle Christmas Annual (1949) p. 44 (S)

_____. "Waiting," Savacou 3/4 (1970/71) p. 142 (P)

Craig, William. Our Lodger. Glasgow: Charles Glass Co.,1895. (B)

Crawford, A.E. Brief Interlude: A Play in the Vernacular in One Scene. [typescript] (D)

Crawford, Robert. "Reverie on Christmas Eve," Chronicle Christmas Annual (1950) p. 50 (S)

Cregan, K.H. "Loser Takes All," Christmas Tide (1935) p. 13 (S)

_____. "The Mark of Hatasu," Christmas Tide (1936) p. 59 (S)

_____. "Salute to Convention," Christmas Tide (1934) p. 47 (S)

_____. "Silver Sands," Christmas Tide (1934) p. 12 (P)

Creole. [Archives 1856-1882 and 1905-1907 incomplete] (X)

Cressall, Nora. From the Caribbean to England in Verse. Ilfracombe, Devon: Stockwell, 1970. *The Wanderer/The Glorious South/The Caribbean Islands/Trinidad/Martinique/Barbados/ Manana/The Spirit of Guyana/Tropic Heat/A Guyana River/Kiskadee/Fever Stricken/Jungle Eyes/Plantation Josie's Song/Humanity!/Britain/Barrage Balloon/Dream/To Frank/London Town (1940-1941)/Poor Old Civilian/Pause a Moment/Fantasy/May 1945/A Friend/Odd-Very Odd/The Tinker/The Request/Isle of Purbeck The Answer/Fickle Memory/Faithless/Narcissus in Reverse/St. James's Park/The Age of Noise/The Bells/The Rover/Beware/Little Lady/Au Revoir/Dreams/They/Love/That's Clear/Avant-Garde!/A Warning/Just Thirteen/The Wick/The Gardener/The Jungle (P)

Crookall, L. British Guiana, Or Work and Wanderings Among the Creoles and Coolies, the Africans and the Indians of the Wild Country. London, 1898. (C,T)

Cruickshank, J. Graham. "Black Talk": Being Notes on Negro Dialect in British Guiana, with (Inevitably) a Chapter on the Vernacular of Barbados. Demerara: Argosy Co., 1916. (L)

26

_____. _Negro Humour, Being Sketches in the Market, on the Road and at My Back Door._ Georgetown: Argosy Co., 1905. (C,L,H)

Cumberbatch, C.E. "A Silver Ship," _Christmas Tide_ (1935) p. 2 (P)

Cundall, Frank. _Bibliography of the West Indies (Excluding Jamaica),_ Kingston: The Institute of Jamaica, 1909. New York: London: Johnson Reprint Corp., 1971. (Z)

Cunningham, William. "A Son of the Soil," _Christmas Tide_ (1923) p. 23 (S)

D

D, E.M. "Timber from Guiana," _Christmas Tide_ (1948) p. 18 (P)

Dabydeen, Cyril. *Crack of Dawn p. 12/Driftwood p. 11/Fisherman p. 13/Moonlight p. 11/Oarsman p. 10/Song of Praise p. 10/Sunlight p. 13 _Kaie_ 5 (1968) (P)

_____. "A Dream," _New World_ (Fortnightly) 4 (1964) p. 27 (P)

_____. "Evening," _New World_ (Fortnightly) 16 (1965) p. 22 (P)

_____. "My Dead," _New World_ (Fortnightly) 3 (1964) p. 24 (P)

_____. "One Day," _New World_ (Fortnightly) 3 (1964) p. 23 (P)

_____. "Poem to Your Own," _Kaie_ 6 (1970) p. 29 (P)

_____. _Poems in Recession._ Georgetown: Sheik Sadeek, 1972. *To Love My Country/Questing Spirit/Rain/Moonlight/In the Slumber of Night/Orchids/The Miracle Day/On Looking from a Tower/Sinews/Fisherman/Driftwood/Hogstye/Poem to Your Own/My Dead/Ode to Cuffy/Heiroglyph [sic]/The Orchard/Listening to Trees/The Village Sound/Of Trees and You/Poem for a Child (P)

_____. "Reality," _New World_ (Fortnightly) 27/28 (1965) p. 38 also _Kaie_ 2 (1966) p. 47 (P)

_____. "Single Episode," p. 7 Trotman's _Voices_ (P)

_____. "To Love My Country," _New World_ (Fortnightly) 27/28 (1965) p. 38 also _Kaie_ 2 (1966) p. 46 (P)

_____. "Wet Streets," _New World_ (Fortnightly) 12 (1965) p. 4 also _Kaie_ 2 (1966) p. 48 (P)

Da Costa, Richard. "A Birthday Present," _Kaie_ 5 (1968) p. 28 (P)

The Daily Argosy. [Archives 1926-1960; few issues missing; _Daily Argosy_ ceased publ. 1961; _Sunday Argosy_ ceased 1963] (X)

The Daily Chronicle. One of two Georgetown dailies currently being published; Government-owned [Archives 1885-1960; few issues missing] (X)

Daily Liberal. [Archives 1891-1894 incomplete] (X)

Dalton, (Dr.) Henry G. *The Carib's Complaint p. 93/The Essequibo and Its Tributaries p. 25/The Lamaha p. 77/Lines Written After Seeing the Falls of Niagara p. 79 Cameron's Guianese Poetry... (P)

_____. Tropical Lays and Other Poems. 1853. (P)

Daly, P.H. "The Arrest," Kyk-Over-Al 13 (1951) p. 191 [extract from unpublished novel] (N-e)

_____. "The Death of Quamina," Kyk-Over-Al 17 (1953) p. 210 (N-e)

_____. "Our Heritage," Christmas Tide (1934) p. 40 (P)

_____. Revolution to Republic. Georgetown: Daily Chronicle, 1970. (C)

_____. Story of the Heroes. Georgetown: Daily Chronicle, Book I, 1940; Book II, 1941; Book III, 1943. (B)

_____. "Walter MacArthur Lawrence," Kyk-Over-Al 2 (1946) p. 18 (E)

_____. West Indian Freedom and West Indian Literature. Georgetown: Daily Chronicle, 1951. (E)

_____. [cf. Lawrence, Walter MacArthur--The Poet of Guiana...]

_____. [cf. Seymour, A.J.--"Is There a West Indian Way of Life?"]

Daly, Vere Trevelyan. "Brilliant Marriage," Christmas Tide (1936) p. 86 (S)

_____. "Consistency," Christmas Tide (1934) p. 54 (P)

_____. "The Happy Medium," Christmas Tide (1935) p. 47 (S)

_____. "Historical Background to the Co-Operative Republic," p. 211 Searwar's Co-Operative Republic (C)

_____. "Hymn for Guyana's Children," p. 34 A New Guyana (P)

_____. The Making of Guyana. London: Macmillan, 1974. (C)

_____. "A Song in Season," Christmas Tide (1935) p. 46 (P)

_____. "The Song of Young Guiana," p. 111 Cameron's Guianese Poetry... (P)

_____. "The Story of Kykoveral," Kyk-Over-Al 1 (1945) p. 18 (C)

Dalzell, Frank E. "Attunement of the Senses," Kyk-Over-Al 3 (1946) p. 12 (P)

_____. "Caribbean Call," Christmas Tide (1950) p. 4 (P)

_____. "A Dawn Shall Break," Christmas Tide (1947) p. 8 (S)

_____. "Emerald Isle," Kyk-Over-Al (1945) p. 12 (P)

_____. "Guianese Coastland," <u>Kyk-Over-Al</u> 6 (1948) p. 7 (P)

_____. "The Kiskadee," <u>Kyk-Over-Al</u> 19 (1954) p. 93 also p. 49 Seymour's <u>My Lovely Native Land</u> also p. 16 Seymour's <u>Fourteen Guianese Poems for Children</u> also p. 38 Seymour's <u>Themes of Song</u> also p. 57 Elma Seymour's <u>Sun is a Shapely Fire</u> (P)

_____. "Lawrie 'Wakes' No more," <u>Caribia</u> (1952/53) p. 1 (S)

_____. "Lines to a Spinster," <u>Kyk-Over-Al</u> 2 (1946) p. 9 (P)

_____. "Men Are Such Suckers," <u>Chronicle Christmas Annual</u> (1946) p. 12 (S)

_____. <u>Moments of Leisure</u>. British Guiana, 1952. [Miniature Poet Series] *Guiana's Voice/Stabroek Square/The River Demerara/The Kiskadee/To Gena/When I Have Ceased to Be/My Secret Loves/Lines to a Spinster/Obituary of a Bum/Attunement of the Senses/To Youth/Caribbean Call/Deserted Cottage (P)

_____. "The Mystic Touch," p. 32 Elma Seymour's <u>Sun is a Shapely Fire</u> (P)

_____. "Obituary of a Bum," <u>Kyk-Over-Al</u> 4 (1947) p. 8 also 19 (1954) p. 86 (P)

_____. "The River Demerara," <u>Kyk-Over-Al</u> 19 (1954) p. 70 also p. 14 Seymour's <u>Fourteen Guianese Poems for Children</u> also p. 17 Seymour's <u>Themes of Song</u> also p. 15 Elma Seymour's <u>Sun is a Shapely Fire</u> (P)

_____. "Signs of the Times," <u>Chronicle Christmas Annual</u> (1947) p. 41 (P)

_____. "Turn Back the Clock," <u>Christmas Tide</u> (1947) p. 4 (P)

Daniels, Wilfred. "All I Can See," <u>Kaie</u> 10 (1973) p. 36 (P)

Darlson, Winifred. (pseud.?) "He Wanted 'Em Different," <u>Caribia</u> (1952/53) p. 35 (S)

Das, Mahadai. "Me An' Melda," p. 1 Monar's <u>Poems for Guyanese Children</u> (P)

_____. "Mystery of the Night," Gora Singh's <u>Heritage</u> (P)

_____. "There You Lie," Gora Singh's <u>Heritage</u> (P)

Dash, McDonald. *Greenheart Man p. 65/Pieces p. 66 Seymour's <u>New Writing in the Caribbean</u> (P)

Dathorne, Oscar Ronald. "Africa in the Literature of the West Indies," <u>Journal of Commonwealth Literature</u> 1 (1965) p. 95 (E)

_____. "The African Novel: Document to Experiment," <u>Bulletin of the Association for African Literature in English</u> 3 (1965) p. 18 (E)

_____. (ed.) <u>African Poetry for Schools and Colleges</u>. London: Macmillan, 1969. (P)

_____. The Black Mind. A History of African Literature. Minneapolis: Univ. of Minnesota, 1975. (Cr)

_____. (ed.) Caribbean Narrative. London: Heinemann,1966.(Y)

_____. (ed.) Caribbean Verse; an Anthology. London: Heinemann, 1967. (P)

_____. "Constable," Black Orpheus 17 (1965) p. 18 (S)

_____. Dumplings in the Soup. London: Cassell, 1963. (N)

_____. "Guyanisation of Hodge," p. 199 Seymour's New Writing in the Caribbean (S)

_____. "Letter from Lagos," p. 66 Sergeant's New Voices of the Commonwealth (P)

_____. "Poem of Exile," p. 28 Thieme's Anthology of West Indian Literature also p. 160 Sergeant's Commonwealth Poems of Today (P)

_____. "Roger Mais: The Man on the Cross," SNNTS 4 p. 275 (E)

_____. The Scholar Man. London: Cassell, 1964. (N)

_____. "The Wintering of Mr. Kolawole," p. 223 Salkey's Stories from the Caribbean (S)

_____. "The Writers of Guyana," The Times Literary Supplement (26 May 1966) p. 480 (E)

_____ and Willfried Feuser. (eds.) Africa in Prose. Baltimore: Penguin, 1969. (Y)

Davies, J. "High Tide," Chronicle Christmas Annual (1961) p. 33 (S)

Davis, Leslie C. *Alphecca p. 107/Day of Delight p. 90/Flowers for You p. 109/Satan's Serenade p. 127 Kyk-Over-Al 19 (1954) (P)

_____. Eternal Tribute. British Guiana, 1958. *To Winston Churchill/To Benito Mussolini/While the Bombs Fell/The Sighing Sea/Prayer for Old World/Britain's Immortal Poetry/Lines to an English Authoress/A Song of the Commonwealth's Children/Eternal Tribute/Creation/Let Us Have Peace (P)

_____. Invocation to Sivananda. British Guiana: Adana Printing Service, 1957. *Satan's Serenade/Vision/Invocation to Sivananda/The Sick Poet's Sorrow (P)

Davson, Victor. "You Could Never," p. 13 R.C. McAndrew's Plexus (S)

Dawn. Annandale, E.C.D. (Georgetown), Guyana [1st issue appeared 1973] (J)

De Abreu, Ronald. "The Leader," Expression I (1966) p. 21 (P)

De Cambra, H. Leslie. Don Paula. London: Stockwell, n.d. (N?)

30

Debidiu, Ada E.B. "Lines at Bartica," <u>Chronicle Christmas Annual</u> (1967) p. 37 (P)

de Goeje, C.H. "Anansi, l'araignée rusée," [Anansi, the wily spider] <u>Revta Mus Paul</u> new ser. 1 (1947) p. 125 (F)

_____. <u>Curiositeiten uit Guyana</u>. 1934/35. (F)

_____. <u>Philosophy, Initiation and Myths of the Indians of Guiana and Adjacent Countries</u>. 1943. (F)

_____. <u>The Physical World, the World of Magic, and the Moral World of Guiana Indians</u>. 1952. (F)

de Jonge, Laurie. *I Affirm God's Presence is Here. p. 124/Man Know Thyself p. 123/Meditation p. 123 <u>Kyk-Over-Al</u> 19 (1954) (P)

<u>Demba Digest</u>. publ. every 3 weeks by Demerara Bauxite Co., Linden, Guyana [continues <u>MacKenzie Miner</u>; continued by <u>Guybau News</u>] (J)

Delph, Christine A. "Echoes of the Past," <u>Chronicle Christmas Annual</u> (1952) p. 46 (S)

Delph, Malcolm. "If You Wish Let Us Make a Dream," <u>Kyk-Over-Al</u> 16 (1953) p. 161 [transcreation of a Victor Hugo poem] (P)

<u>The Demerara Daily Chronicle</u>. [Archives 1881-1884 incomplete] (X)

<u>The Demerara Times</u>. [Archives 1875-1876 incomplete] (X)

Dempster, Carl O. "The Unwilling Communist," <u>Chronicle Christmas Annual</u> (1950) p. 57 (S)

Denny, Zivic M. "The Slave Converts," <u>Chronicle Christmas Annual</u> (1957) p. 29 (S)

de Peana, George. <u>As I See It</u>. Georgetown: author, 1972 [13 articles] (E)

De Souza, Michael G. "Happy Christmas," <u>Chronicle Christmas Annual</u> (1958) p. 6 (S)

Des Voeux, (Sir) William. <u>Experiences of a Demerara Magistrate, 1865-1870</u>. [reprinted as No. 11 in Daily Chronicle Guiana Edition Series, Georgetown, 1948; ed. Vincent Roth] (A)

_____. <u>My Colonial Service in British Guiana, St. Lucia, Trinidad, Fiji, Newfoundland, and Hong Kong, with Interludes</u>. Vols. I and II. London: J. Murray, 1903. (A)

de Villiers, J.A.J. [cf. Gravesande, Laurens Storm van 's]

Dewar, Lilian. "Jamaica in the Novel," <u>Kyk-Over-Al</u> 12 (1951) p. 108 (E)

de Weever, Jacqueline. "The Artifice of Eternity," <u>Kyk-Over-Al</u> 16 (1953) p. 152 (E)

_____. "The Dancer," <u>Kyk-Over-Al</u> 23 (1958) p. 27 (S)

_____. "Four Poems." *Foreign Morning p. 6/Poem [Your sweet brown fingers weave for me] p. 7/Riches p. 6/Sun-Song p. 7 Kyk-Over-Al 26 (1959) (P)

_____. "The Madrigal," Kyk-Over-Al 26 (1959) p. 21 (S)

_____. *Poem [In a skirt of gentle breezes] p. 100/Poem [When new moon's pallor blushes in the sky] p. 104 Kyk-Over-Al 19 (1954) (P)

_____. "The Rice Fairies," p. 113 Seymour's My Lovely Native Land (F)

_____. "Song," Kyk-Over-Al 20 (1955) p. 146 (P)

Dharaupaul, Cecilia. "Bushrum," Kaie 8 (1971) p. 51 (S)

Dick, Red. (pseud.) "Love Frustrated," Chronicle Christmas Annual (1949) p. 28 (S)

_____. "Natural Increase," Chronicle Christmas Annual (1950) p. 21 (S)

_____. "Transition," Chronicle Christmas Annual (1947) p. 2 (S)

Diocesan Magazine. [Georgetown, publ. monthly] (X)

D'Oliveira, Evadne. "Anticipation," Chronicle Christmas Annual (1966) p. 132 (P)

_____. "A Day at 63," Chronicle Christmas Annual (1967) p. 136 (P)

_____. "Drama at Tukeit" [broadcast B.B.C. 1968 under title "The Choice"] (S)

_____. The Female of the Species: A Play for Radio. [typescript] (D)

_____. *The Hiatus of Pride p. 33/The Language of Inadequacy p. 32/On the Brink p. 30/Potaro p. 29/Shall We Survive p. 35/ Tukeit p. 31/What Sad Songs p. 34 Douglas' Guyana Drums (P)

_____. If Freedom Fails: A Play for Radio. [typescript] (D)

_____. "Kaieteur," Chronicle Christmas Annual (1967) p. 78 (P)

_____. "The Rights of Man," p. 10 Trotman's Voices of Guyana (P)

_____. The Scattered Jewels. perf. Georgetown and Mackenzie (Linden) 1969 (D)

_____. The Shadow and the Substance. [typescript] (D)

_____. "Symphony," Chronicle Christmas Annual (1966) p. 137 (P)

_____. "Tukeit," Kaie 5 (1968) p. 19 (P)

_____. "When the Poet Sings," Chronicle Christmas Annual (1967) p. 79 (P)

_____. [included in Stories from Guyana, 1967; produced by six writers for Canada's Expo '67]

D'Oliveira, Jocelyn. "Mine Own Guiana," Chronicle Christmas
  Annual (1946) p. 28 (P)
_____. [cf. Seymour, A.J.--"Greatness and Bitterness"]
Dolphin, Celeste. "Arawak Rhythm," Caribia (1945) p. 33 (S)
_____. Children of Guiana. Georgetown, 1953. [series of
  broadcasts--Radio Demerara 1953] (C)
_____. "Christmas Carol," Chronicle Christmas Annual (1949)
  p. 18 (S)
_____. "Essential Service," Chronicle Christmas Annual (1948)
  p. 29 (S)
_____. "The Little Chinese Boy," p. 92 Seymour's My Lovely
  Native Land [extract from Children of Guiana] (C)
_____. "My Cousin Renée," Chronicle Christmas Annual (1945)
  p. 41 (S)
_____. "The Poetry of A.J. Seymour," New World (Fortnightly)
  13 (1965) p. 31 (E)
_____. "Portrait of J.G.," Caribia (1946/47) p. 66 (S)
_____. "Trouble Music," Kyk-Over-Al 8 (1949) p. 21 (S)
_____ and A.J. Seymour. "The Genius of Place: Personal An-
  thology of Poetry from the British Commonwealth," Kyk-Over-Al
  16 (1953) p. 170 [a British Council Broadcast] (E)
Dolphin, Lynette. (comp.) Ten National Songs of Guyana. George-
  town: The National History and Arts Council, 1969. [includes
  Guyana National Anthem, words by A.L. Luker, music by R.C.G.
  Potter] (Mu)
Don, Thomas. *Bless'd Surety of the Human Race p. 174/Lines
  from 'Jehovah, the Saviour of Mankind' p. 173/A Night Prayer
  p. 175/O! Sweet Saviour p. 172/The Rich, Poor Man and the Poor,
  Rich Man p. 176/The Sabbath-Keeper p. 173 Cameron's Guianese
  Poetry... (P)
_____. Pious Effusions. 1873. (P)
Doris, Errol. (ed.) Creation: Works of Art. Georgetown, 1972. (Y)
Douglas, Syble G. "The Bread of Life," p. 25 Elma Seymour's
  Sun is a Shapely Fire (P)
_____. Fulfilment. Poems. Georgetown, 1967. *The Bread of
  Life/These to Cherish/Sudden Death/Twilight/The Scars of Liv-
  ing/Bad Patch/Thanksgiving/Fulfilment (A Journey Through
  Time) (P)
_____. (ed.) Guyana Drums. Georgetown, 1972. *The Return
  p. 5/Guyana Drums p. 6/To a Tree at '63' p. 10/Beside the
  Wall p. 12 [five other women poets included in this anthol-
  ogy published for Carifesta '72: Pat Cameron, Sheila King,
  Evadne D'Oliveira, Mitzie Townshend, and Shana Yardan] (P)
_____. "In Memorian," p. 8 Trotman's Voices of Guyana (P)

_____. "The Return," p. 20 <u>A New Guyana</u> (P)

Drakes, S.A. <u>The Dead End</u>. perf. Guyana 1963 (D)

Drayton, E.S. "French Refugee," <u>Caribia</u> (1945) p. 40 (S)

Drepaul, Joseph. *The Dead Leaf p. 23/An End p. 4 R.C. McAndrew's
   <u>Plexus</u> (S)

Drepaul, Michael. [cf. <u>Expression</u>; Drepaul and Brian Chan ed.
   <u>Expression 4</u>, 1968]

_____. [cf. <u>Expression</u>; Drepaul and N.D. Williams ed. <u>Expres-</u>
   <u>sion 2</u> and 3½]

Dummett, Joan. "A Guyanese National Theatre?" Part I = <u>New World</u>
   (Fortnightly) 24 (1965) p. 12, Part II = 25 (1965) p. 15, Part
   III = 26 (1965) p. 13 [panel discussion Georgetown, May, 1965,
   with Neville Robinson, Pat Clarke, Nelo Adams, Joyce Trotman,
   Pat Anderson, Helen Taitt, Sheik Sadeek, Ashton Phillips, Ken
   Corsbie, Claudette Jones, Vibert Parvattan, and Joan Dummett] (S)

Dumont, Cyril N. "The Jade Casket," <u>Christmas Tide</u> (1936) p. 38 (S)

Dunn, James. <u>Glints of Guiana</u>. New Amsterdam, British Guiana:
   The Lutheran Press, 1938. (F)

Dutch Correspondence in the National Archives of Guyana, 1784-
   1935. [consists of correspondence in Dutch of the Dutch West
   India Company and the States General of the United Netherlands
   to 1803; from 1803, the correspondence is that of the Government (later, Colonial) Secretary's Office; letter books, dis-
   patches, files] (Co)

E

<u>Echo</u>. [Archives 1887-1899 incomplete] (X)

Edun, Ayube M. <u>London's Heart-Probe and Britain's Destiny</u>.
   London: Arthur H. Stockwell, 19-? (A,T)

Elliott, T.R.F. *Emancipation Chorus p. 142/Jubilee Carol p. 145/
   Rejoice! 'Tis Freedom's Jubilee p. 144/Thanksgiving p. 143
   Cameron's <u>Guianese Poetry...</u> (P)

<u>Emery's Journal</u>. [Archives 1847] (X)

Engber, Marjorie. (comp.) <u>Caribbean Fiction and Poetry</u>. New
   York: Center for Inter-American Relations, 1970. [bibliog-
   raphy arranged by genre, indexed by authors, titles, coun-
   tries] (Z)

<u>Essequibo and Demerary Gazette.</u> [Archives 1803-1813 incom-
   plete] (X)

Essequibo and Demerary Royal Gazette. [Archives 1807-1813 in-
    complete] (X)

Etwaru, Arnold. "Drought," Kaie 5 (1968) p. 22 also Chronicle
    Christmas Annual (1967) p. 77 also Poet 13,1 (1972) p. 10 (P)

_____. "I Will Call You Back," Kaie 5 (1968) p. 15 (P)

_____. "Individual Legends," Kaie 5 (1968) p. 14 (P)

_____. "One Day," Chronicle Christmas Annual (1967) p. 78 (P)

_____. "Retrospect," Kaie 5 (1968) p. 23 (P)

Evans, W.W. Memoirs of the Lives of Eminent Man of the Negro
    Race. Georgetown, 1908. (B)

Evening Post. [publ. Georgetown with Weekend Post and Sunday
    Argosy] (X)

Evelyn-Moe, L. [pseud. = Uncle Stapie] "Topics of the Times--
    Uncle Stapie 'pon de People." [a popular column of Creolese
    writing which appeared in every Sunday Argosy in Georgetown
    between 1931-1945] (C,L,H)

Expression. Georgetown. [began 1966 as Expression I, journal
    of poems of students; continued Expression 2, 1967; Expres-
    sion 3½, 1967; and Expression 4, 1968 as "an independent
    literary magazine"; also cf. Lowe, Janice--Expression
    Six] (J,Y)

F

Farabee, William Curtis. The Central Arawaks. The Netherlands:
    Anthropological Publications, 1967. [orig. publ. Univ. of
    Pennsylvania, 1918] (F,C)

Farley, Seville. Blood-Thirsty: A Play in One Scene. [type-
    script] (D)

_____. Jarge-town: A Play in the Vernacular in One Scene.
    [typescript] (D)

Farr, Totem. (pseud.) "Taking Life Easy," Caribia (1949/50)
    p. 78 (S)

Farrier, C.A. Guyanese Humour Store #2. Georgetown: C.A.
    Welshman. n.d. (M,H)

Farrier, Francis Quamina. Air Partner: A Play in the Vernacular
    in One Act. perf. Georgetown: Theatre Guild 1963. (D)

_____. Backward March. broadcast Radio Demerara 1970 [half-
    hour radio play with stage version] (D)

_____. Border Bridge: A Play in One Act. perf. Georgetown: Theatre Guild 1963 [also broadcast Radio Demerara 1970] (D)

_____. Chippy. broadcast Radio Demerara 1970 (D)

_____. Echoes of the Savannahs. broadcast Radio Demerara 1970 (D)

_____. Eyes. broadcast Radio Demerara 1970 (D)

_____. A Family Christmas: A Thirty-Minute Play for Radio. broadcast 1964 (D)

_____. Freedom Trail. broadcast Guyana Broadcasting Service 1971 [also a one-act stage play] (D)

_____. Fugitive from the Royal Jail. broadcast Radio Demerara 1970 (D)

_____. Game. broadcast Radio Demerara 1970 (D)

_____. Gaylanda. perf. 1966 [three-act musical comedy] (D,Mu

_____. The Girl from Susanburg. broadcast Radio Demerara 1968 [radio serial; sequel to The Tides of Susanburg; cf. below] (D)

_____. Home is for Christmas: A Play in the Vernacular for Radio in One Act. broadcast 1964 (D)

_____. In Memorial. broadcast Radio Demerara 1965 (D)

_____. Land of Beautiful Daughters. broadcast Radio Demerara 1970 (D)

_____. Loafers' Lane. broadcast 1967 [also stage version] (D

_____. Manaka: A Play in One Act. perf. Georgetown: Theatre Guild 1965 (D)

_____. Opportunity. broadcast Radio Demerara 1970 (D)

_____. Pal: A One-Act Play. perf. Georgetown: Theatre Guild 1963 (D)

_____. The Plight of the Wright. Georgetown: author, 1969. [perf. Georgetown: The Dramatic Core 1966] (D)

_____. Quitters: A Play in One Act. perf. Georgetown: Theatre Guild 1965 (D)

_____. Rigor Mortis. broadcast Radio Demerara 1970 (D)

_____. Sky Rocket. broadcast Radio Demerara 1970 (D)

_____. The Slave and the Scroll: A Play in One Act. Georgetown: author, 1970. [perf. Georgetown: Theatre Guild 1964] (D)

_____. Something to Live For. broadcast 1967 (D)

_____. The Tides of Susanburg. broadcast Radio Demerara 1966 [radio serial; cf. above sequel: The Girl from Susanburg] (D)

_____. Timberline. broadcast Radio Demerara 1970 (D)

_____. _To Catch a Desperado_. broadcast Radio Demerara 1970 (D)

_____. _A Walk in the Night_. broadcast Radio Demerara 1970 (D)

_____. _With Strings_. broadcast Radio Demerara 1970 (D)

_____. _Zingay_. broadcast Radio Demerara 1970 (D)

Ferdinand, J.E. "The First Prize Story," _Chronicle Christmas Annual_ (1967) p. 19 (S)

Fernandes, J. Leonard. "A Bargain's a Bargain," _Chronicle Christmas Annual_ (1947) p. 15 (S)

_____. "He Had to Be a Hero," _Christmas Tide_ (1949) p. 37 (S)

_____. "Knight-Errant at Large," _Christmas Tide_ (1947) p. 11 (S)

_____. "Mr. Briggs' Lucky Day," _Christmas Tide_ (1934) p. 64 (S)

_____. "Mr. Popham Presses His Suit," _Chronicle Christmas Annual_ (1952) p. 31 (S)

Ferreira, Albert S. "Before Dark," _Chronicle Christmas Annual_ (1945) p. 35 (S)

_____. "Handful of Hibiscus," _Chronicle Christmas Annual_ (1950) p. 2 (S)

_____. "Lullaby for Libby," _Caribia_ (1948/49) p. 9 (S)

_____. "November Day," _Chronicle Christmas Annual_ (1953) p. 4 (S)

_____. "Remember Me to Robie," _Caribia_ (1949/50) p. 23 (S)

_____. "Sign Off," _Caribia_ (1947/48) p. 9 (S)

_____. _A Sonata is Simple_. Georgetown: B.G. Lithographic Co., 1946. (N)

_____. "Speaking on the Sun," _Chronicle Christmas Annual_ (1947) p. 20 (S)

_____. "Time Was When," _Christmas Tide_ (1949) p. 66 (S)

Field-Ridley, Jean. *O Hell Hell p. 13/Mosquitoes p. 28 _Expression I_ (1966) (P)

Figueira, Cyril R. "Somebody's Mother," _Chronicle Christmas Annual_ (1952) p. 29 (S)

_____. "Total Recall," _Chronicle Christmas Annual_ (1949) p. 55 (S)

_____. "Tragic Triangle," _Chronicle Christmas Annual_ (1950) p. 66 (S)

_____. "You Owe Me One," _Chronicle Christmas Annual_ (1951) p. 19 (S)

Figueroa, John. (ed.) _Caribbean Voices_. Vol. I: _Dreams and Visions_. London: Evans, 1966. Vol. II: _The Blue Horizons_.

London: Evans, 1970. combined edition: London: Evans, 1971. (Y)

For the Fighting Front: An Anthology of Revolutionary Poems: A Special Edition for the 8th PYO Festival Congress, 13th-15th April 1974. Georgetown: PYO, 1974. (P)

Ford, Felix. (pseud. ?) "Cassius from Bondage," Caribia (1948/49) p. 15 (S)

Forde, A.N. (ed.) Talk of the Tamarinds: An Anthology of Poetry for Secondary Schools. London: Edward Arnold; Trinidad: Columbus Publishers, 1971. (P)

Forrester, Ivan. *Belizean Girl p. 74/Delinquents p. 69/Etanami p. 70/A Man, the River or the Wind p. 68/Mazaruni p. 72 Seymour's New Writing in the Caribbean (P)

Forsythe, Victor. Liberty Village: A Play for Radio. broadcast 1966 (D)

_____. Sweet Carilla: A Thirty Minute Play Written for Radio. broadcast 1958; stage version perf. Guyana 1961 (D)

_____. The Water Front. broadcast Radio Demerara 1970 (D)

Foster, D. "There's More Music in the Sky," Kaie 6 (1970) p. 28 (P)

Fraser, Alvin. "The Elusive Lady," Chronicle Christmas Annual (1953) p. 28 (S)

Fraser, Louise. "I Was A Cumfa Dancer," Chronicle Christmas Annual (1946) p. 19 (S)

Fraser, Winslow. Andel: A Play in One Act. [typescript] (D)

_____. Auntie Annette: A Play in One Act. perf. Guyana (1959?) (D)

_____. Backward Turn Backwards: A Play in Two Acts. 1969 [typescript] (D)

_____. Bacra Dead ah Backdam: A Play in One Act. [typescript] (D)

_____. Black Sheep. 1965 [typescript] (D)

_____. Body in the Lamaha: A Play in Two Acts. [typescript] (D)

_____. Death Cell 13: A Play in One Act. [typescript] (D)

_____. Death Dream of Cassell Barry. perf. Guyana 1971 (D)

_____. Death Was the Bridegroom: A Play in One Act. [typescript] (D)

_____. Forbidden Love. [typescript] (D)

_____. Home from Onderneeming. 1966 [typescript] (D)

_____. In a Co-Op Republic: A Play. [typescript] (D)

_____. Inside the Forum: A Sketch. perf. Guyana 1958 (D)

_____. Life is But an Empty Dream: A Play in Two Acts. perf. Guyana 1970 (D)

_____. Murder in the Playhouse: A Play in Three Acts. 1970 [typescript] (D)

_____. No. 55 Wildroot Alley: A Play in One Act. perf. Guyana (1965?) (D)

_____. Our Last Job. [typescript] (D)

_____. Professor John: A Play in One Act. perf. Guyana 1963 (D)

_____. Ramona: A Play in Three Acts. [typescript] (D)

_____. Strange Secret. perf Guyana 1965 [typescript] (D)

_____. Trouble at Arvida: A Play. 1971 [typescript] (D)

_____. Valley of Tears: A Play in 4 Acts. perf. 1969 [typescript] (D)

_____. Village Delinquent: A Play in Two Acts. perf. Guyana 1968 (D)

_____. Winds of Change: A Play. perf. Guyana 1971 (D)

Fredericks, Patrick A. "Memory of the Burning Sun," Kaie 8 (1971) p. 90 (S)

Freedomways. 4, 3 (1964) [special West Indian no.] (J)

G

G., J. [John Gale?] "Exchange of Letters. Standards of Criticism," Kyk-Over-Al 25 (1959) p. 111 (E)

_____. [cf. Seymour, A.J.--"Greatness and Bitterness"]

Gajraj, R.B. (ed.) The Guiana East Indian Christmas Number. Georgetown: M. Akbar, 1938. (C)

Galperina, Eugenie. (ed.) The Time of Flambouy Trees: An Anthology of West Indian Poetry. Moscow, 1961. (P)

Ganie, Alfred S. "Coins for the Cripple," Chronicle Christmas Annual (1957) p. 15 (S)

Gardner, Kenneth M. "The Christmas Card," Chronicle Christmas Annual (1958) p. 13 (S)

Gentles, Hugh. "Evenin' Time," New World Quarterly 2,2 (1966) p. 41 (S)

Giddings, (Rev.) P. Quid Rides (Why Do You Laugh?): A Collection of Ten Sketches. 1893. (D)

Gilkes, Michael. "The Art of Extremity--Wilson Harris' <u>Ascent to Omai</u>," <u>Caribbean Quarterly</u> 17, 3 and 4 (1971) p. 83 (E)

_____. <u>Couvade</u>. London: Longmans Caribbean, 1975. (D)

_____. <u>In Transit</u>. perf. Georgetown: Theatre Guild, 1969 (D)

_____. <u>Racial Identity and Individual Consciousness in the Caribbean Novel</u>. [text of 1974 Edgar Mittelholzer Memorial Lectures] (E)

_____. "The Role of Drama in the University," <u>New World Quarterly</u> 2,2 (1969) p. 3 (E)

_____. "The Spirit in the Bottle: A Reading of Mittelholzer's <u>A Morning at the Office</u>," <u>World Literature Written in English</u> 14,1 (1975) p. 237 (E)

_____. <u>Wilson Harris and the Caribbean Novel</u>. London: Longman Caribbean, 1975. (Cr.)

Gimble, Rosemary. <u>Jonathon and Large</u>. London: Andre Deutsch, 1965. (N)

<u>GISRA</u> [Guyana Institute for Social Research and Action] Georgetown. [Vol. 1, No. 1 publ. March 1970. 4 issues per year] (J)

Gittens, Joyce. (pseud.?) "Someone Died," <u>Caribia</u> (1946/47) p. 125 (S)

_____. "Those Who Find," <u>Caribia</u> (1947/48) p. 45 (S)

Giuseppi, Neville and Undine Giuseppi. (comps.) <u>Backfire. A Collection of Short Stories from the Caribbean for Use in Secondary Schools</u>. London: Macmillan, 1973. (S)

Glen, Ignatius. *Lulu Water p. 112/Mineena p. 72/The River in October p. 96 <u>Kyk-Over-Al</u> 19 (1954) (P)

Gomes, Clement A. [pseud. = Cob Cotton] "Not the Same," p. 123 Cameron's <u>Guianese Poetry...</u> (P)

_____. "One Sunday Afternoon," <u>Christmas Tide</u> (1936) p. 78 (S)

_____. "Smart Fish to the Ladies," <u>Caribia</u> (1945) p. 31 (S)

Gomes, Joan Mavis. "As Ithers See Us," <u>Chronicle Christmas Annual</u> (1946) (S)

Gonsalves, Effie. "A Prayer for Peace," <u>Christmas Tide</u> (1935) p. 23 (P)

Gonsalves, M. "The Kanaima," <u>Christmas Tide</u> (1948) p. 28 (S)

Gonsalves, Reginald. "Christmas Tide," <u>Christmas Tide</u> (1923) p. 16 (P)

Goodall, Edward. "Diary of Edward Goodall During His Sojourn in Georgetown from 28th July to 11th December 1844," <u>Journal of the British Guiana Museum and Zoo</u> 35 (1962) p. 39; 36 (1962) p. 47 (A)

Goodwin, K.L. (ed.) <u>National Identity. Papers Delivered at the</u>
<u>Commonwealth Literature Conference, University of Queenland,</u>
<u>Brisbane, 9-15 August, 1968</u>. London, Melbourne: Heinemann,
1970. (E)

Gordon, Jack J. "The Last Haul," <u>Chronicle Christmas Annual</u>
(1947) p. 17 (S)

Goring, George Ingram. "The Manatee," p. 58 Elma Seymour's <u>Sun</u>
<u>Is a Shapely Fire</u> (P)

_____. "Raleigh Had a Daughter," <u>Chronicle Christmas Annual</u>
(1952) p. 9 (S)

Goveia, E.V. <u>The West Indian Slave Laws of the 18th Century</u>.
Barbados: Caribbean Universities Press, 1970. [publ. with
C.J. Bartlett's <u>A New Balance of Power: The 19th Century</u>] (C)

Grange, Peter. [pseud. cf. Nicole, Christopher]

Grant, Cedric. <u>Company Towns in the Caribbean</u>. Georgetown:
Ministry of Information, 1971. (C)

Grant, Cy. "Loneliness," p. 96 Figueroa's <u>Caribbean Voices</u> (P)

Grant, Harold. "Good for Nothing Rubbish," <u>Chronicle Christmas</u>
<u>Annual</u> (1961) p. 16 (S)

Gravesande, Laurens Storm van 's. <u>The Rise of British Guiana</u>.
London: Hakluyt Society, 1911. 2 vols. [compl. from dis-
patches; ed. by C.A. Harris and J.A.J. de Villiers] (C)

Gray, Cecil. (ed.) <u>Bite In. Stage 1</u>. [also <u>Stage 2</u> and <u>Stage 3</u>]
London: Nelson, 1972. (Y)

_____. (ed.) <u>Response</u>. London: Nelson, 1969. (Y)

_____. [cf. Ramchand, Kenneth]

Gray, Henry L. "Kaieteur," <u>Christmas Tide</u> (1935) p. 62 (P)

_____. "The Way of Things," <u>Christmas Tide</u> (1934) p. 71 (S)

Greaves, Stanley. *Strange Fruit p. 5/Trees p. 5 Seymour's <u>Magnet</u> (P)

Green, Jim.(pseud.?) "Garden of Eden," <u>Caribia</u> (1946/47) p. 6 (S)

Green, Leslie. "Reflections," <u>Chronicle Christmas Annual</u> (1951)
p. 13 (S)

Greene, Eustace. [pseud. cf. Monar, M.R.]

Griffith, Cecil C. <u>Within Four Walls</u>. Georgetown, 1971. (A)

Grimes, John. "Elise," <u>Kyk-Over-Al</u> 6 (1948) p. 3 and 19 (1954)
p. 102 (P)

_____. "Panacea," <u>Chronicle Christmas Annual</u> (1946) p. 28 (P)

Grimshaw, Thelma. "High School Interlude," <u>Chronicle Christmas</u>
<u>Annual</u> (1955) p. 13 (S)

<u>Guiana Chronicle</u>. [Archives 1822-1845 incomplete] (X)

<u>Guiana Chronicle and Demerary Gazette</u>. [Archives 1819-1820 in-
   complete] (X)

<u>Guiana Herald</u>. [Archives 1842-1844 and 1885 incomplete] (X)

<u>Guiana Reformer</u>. [Archives 1840-1841 incomplete] (X)

<u>Guiana Times</u>. [Archives 1840-1866 incomplete] (X)

Gull, C. Ranger. (pseud.) "Poor Old Christmas," <u>Christmas Tide</u>
   (1923) p. 21 (S)

Guppy, N. <u>Wai-Wai</u>. London: Murray, 1958. (C)

<u>Guyana Business</u>. [Georgetown Chamber of Commerce, quarterly] (X)

<u>Guyana Graphic</u>. [one of two Georgetown dailies being published
   currently; Government-owned] (X)

The Guyana Institute for Social Research and Action. [cf. <u>GISRA</u>]

"Guyana National Anthem." [cf. Luker, (Rev.) Archibald L.]

<u>Guyana Observer</u>. [Georgetown, monthly] (X)

<u>Guyanese National Bibliography</u>. [cf. National Library]

<u>Guybau News</u>. [Mackenzie (Linden), Guyana; continues <u>Demba Digest</u>
   fortnightly] (X)

H

H., A. "'Lil,' or the Road I Missed," <u>Chronicle Christmas Annual</u>
   (1950) p. 23 (S)

H., J.E. "Passers-By," <u>Kyk-Over-Al</u> 3 (1946) p. 27 (P)

Hale, Allan. "Bingo Benjy," <u>Chronicle Christmas Annual</u> (1966)
   p. 11 (S)

Hamaludin, Mohamed. <u>Gentlemen-at-Alms: A Play in One Act</u>.
   [typescript] (D)

_____. "The Man and the Marabunta," <u>Chronicle Christmas
   Annual</u> (1967) p. 29 (S)

_____. "The Mother Instinct," <u>Chronicle Christmas Annual</u>
   (1967) p. 39 (S)

_____. <u>Much Married Mary</u>. perf. Guyana 1968 (D)

_____. "No Greater Love," <u>Chronicle Christmas Annual</u> (1967)
   p. 9 (S)

_____. "Red Prints," <u>Chronicle Christmas Annual</u> (1966)
   p. 13 (S)

_____. Whom the Gods Love: A Tragedy in Three Acts. [type-script] (D)

Hamilton, Cleveland Wycliffe. "Helle," Kyk-Over-Al 19 (1954) p. 111 (P)

_____. "Paul Laurence Dunbar," Kyk-Over-Al 7 (1948) p. 17 (E)

_____. R.C.G. Potter. Composer of The Guyana National Anthem. Georgetown. broadcast Guyana Broadcasting Service on Independence Monday, 1968 (B)

_____. "Remembrance Day," Georgetown Sunday Chronicle (10 Nov. 1974) p. 7 (P)

_____. "Symbols," Kyk-Over-Al 9 (1949) p. 4 and 19 (1954) p. 127 (P)

_____. "Thoughts on Crossing the Atlantic," Kyk-Over-Al 15 (1952) p. 70 (P)

Harlequin, Joseph Byron. *Forget-Me-Not p. 104/The Guianese Contingents p. 109/Salvorah Stream--Potaro p. 75 Cameron's Guianese Poetry... (P)

_____. Georgetown--The Garden City of the West. A Description in Verse and Also a Souvenir of the Centenary (1831-1931) of the Union of Berbice with Demerara and Essequibo, Forming the Colony of British Guiana. Georgetown: Persick, 1931. (P)

_____. Lyrics and Other Poems. Georgetown: Daily Chronicle, 1918. *Hope Ever/Contemplation/Christmas, 1903/Love's Invocation/The Two Planets/He Sleeps/Christmas, 1914/Hail to All!/ A Moonlight Tryst/The Return of Peace/Salvorah Stream--Potaro/ The Lesson of Christmas/The Guianese Contingents/Forget-Me-Not (P)

Harewood, Celina. "Wortmanville," Kaie 8 (1971) p. 33 (P)

Harewood, Denys. "If Whimsy Were Enough," Chronicle Christmas Annual (1950) p. 52 (S)

Harewood, Hilton Rupert. "Guiana Miscellany," Empire Digest [Toronto Empire Information] 2, 5 (1945). (M)

Harper, Doris. "Villanelle," Kyk-Over-Al 11 (1950) p. 38 and 19 (1954) p. 98 also p. 31 Seymour's Themes of Song (P)

Harper-Smith, James W. *Luna p. 100/Parchment and Quill p. 126/ To a Dead Silk-Cotton Tree p. 71/Twilight p. 97 Kyk-Over-Al 19 (1954) (P)

_____. Musings. Georgetown, 1951. [Miniature Poet Series] *To Nature/The Rainbow/To Luna/Truant Gold/O Glorious World/ A Poet's Prayer/Twilight/To a Dead Silk-Cotton Tree/Fear/ Meditation and Regret/Poem/A Vesper (P)

_____. "Parchment and Quill," p. 50 Seymour's Themes of Song (P)

_____. "A Poet's Prayer," p. 15 Seymour's <u>Fourteen Guianese Poems for Children</u> also p. 33 Seymour's <u>Themes of Song</u> (P)

_____. "To a Dead Silk-Cotton Tree," <u>Kyk-Over-Al</u> 14 (1952) p. 35 also p. 104 Searwar's <u>Co-Operative Republic</u> also p. 19 Seymour's <u>Themes of Song</u> (P)

_____. "To Luna," p. 29 Seymour's <u>Themes of Song</u> (P)

_____. "Twilight," <u>Kyk-Over-Al</u> 14 (1952) p. 35 also p. 30 Seymour's <u>Themes of Song</u> (P)

Harper-Wills, Doris. "Invocation," p. 7 Seymour's <u>Magnet</u> (P)

_____. "Ole Higue and Young Samaan," <u>Kaie</u> 8 (1971) p. 95 (S)

Harris, C.A. [cf. Gravesande, Laurens Storm van 's]

Harris, George. "I Sat in the Land of Poets," <u>Kyk-Over-Al</u> 19 (1954) p. 121 also p. 49 Seymour's <u>Themes of Song</u> also Seymour's <u>Fourteen Guianese Poems for Children</u> (P)

_____. "Poem," <u>Kyk-Over-Al</u> 7 (1948) p. 4 (P)

Harris, Wilson [Harris, Theodore Wilson]. <u>The Age of the Rainmakers</u>. London: Faber, 1971. *The Age of Kaie/The Mind of Awakaipu/The Laughter of the Wapishanas/Arawak Horizon (S)

_____. "Art and Criticism," <u>Kyk-Over-Al</u> 13 (1951) p. 202 also in Harris' <u>Tradition, the Writer and Society</u>. London: New Beacon, 1967. (E)

_____. <u>Ascent to Omai</u>. London: Faber, 1970. (N)

_____. "Banim Creek," <u>Kyk-Over-Al</u> 18 (1954) p. 36 [extract from unpublished novel] (N-e)

_____. "The Beggar is King (Vindication of Earth)," <u>Kyk-Over-Al</u> 16 (1953) p. 148 also p. 28 Harris's <u>Eternity to Season</u> (P)

_____. <u>Black Marsden</u>. London: Faber, 1972. (N)

_____. "Bouquet for Burrowes," <u>Kyk-Over-Al</u> 18 (1954) p. 8 (E)

_____. "The Canje River," p. 43 Seymour's <u>My Lovely Native Land</u> (

_____. "Charcoal (Epilogue to the Senses: the Heart)," <u>Kyk-Over-Al</u> 22 (1957) p. 25 (P)

_____. "The Chorus," <u>Kyk-Over-Al</u> 19 (1954) p. 128 (P)

_____. "A Comment on <u>A Passage to India</u>," <u>Literary Half-Yearly</u> 10, 2 (1969) (E)

_____. <u>Companions of the Day and Night</u>. London: Faber, 1975. (N

_____. "The Covenant," p. 135 Salkey's <u>West Indian Stories</u> [excerpt from <u>The Far Journey of Oudin</u>] (N-e)

_____. "The Death of Hector, Tamer of Horses," <u>Kyk-Over-Al</u> 22 (1957) p. 23 also <u>Kaie</u> 4 (1967) p. 72 also p. 97 Walmsley's <u>The Sun's Eye</u> (P)

_____. "Denis Williams," Kaie 4 (1967) p. 21 (E)

_____. "The Enigma of Values," New Letters 40, 1 (1973) p. 141 ["open letter to a friend"] (E)

_____. "Eternity to Season. British Guiana: Magnet Printery, 1952. *Troy/Behring Straits/Amazon [publ. under pseud. Kona Waruk] (P)

_____. Eternity to Season (Poems of Separation and Reunion). British Guiana: Master Printery, 1954. Nendeln: Kraus, 1970. *Troy/Behring Straits/Amazon/The Fabulous Well (The quest of home) [6 poems]/The Beggar is King (vindication of earth) [2 poems]/Canje (the river of ocean)/The Spirit of Place [7 poems] (P)

_____. "Extract," p. 213 Seymour's New Writing in the Caribbean [from the "forthcoming" novel Black Marsden] (N-e)

_____. "Extract from a Story," Ariel 1, 1 (1970) p. 43 [from work later entitled The Age of the Rainmakers] (S-e)

_____. The Eye of the Scarecrow. London: Faber, 1965. (N)

_____. "The Fabulous Well," Kyk-Over-Al 15 (1952) p. 48 *The Well (prologues of Creation)/The Mute at the Well (Recreation of the Senses)/The Vision at the Well/The Taste of the Well/ Charcoal/Agamemnon/Rice (Further Prologues of Creation) (P)

_____. The Far Journey of Oudin. London: Faber, 1961. (N)

_____. "The Far Journey of Oudin," New World (1966) p. 89 [Guyana Independence Issue] (N-e)

_____. "Fences Upon the Earth," Kyk-Over-Al 4 (1947) p. 20 (S)

_____. Fetish. British Guiana: Master Printery, 1951. [Miniature Poet Series] *Tropic of Heaven/The Chorus/These Are the Words of an Old Man/Fetish/Orpheus/Voices Only (from the Muse of Lazarus)/Other Dimensions/Vertiges de l'homme (from Tree Above the World) [publ. under pseud. Kona Waruk] (P)

_____. Fossil and Psyche. Austin, Texas: African and Afro-American Studies Research Center, the University of Texas, 1974. (E)

_____. Genesis of the Clowns. London: Faber, 1975. (N)

_____. "Greatness and Bitterness," Kyk-Over-Al 23 (1958) p. 23 (E)

_____. "Green is the Colour of the World 'in Face of Present Being-Buber'," Kyk-Over-Al 6 (1948) p. 7 (P)

_____. "The Guiana Book by A.J. Seymour," Kyk-Over-Al 7 (1948) p. 37 (E)

_____. Heartland. London: Faber, 1964. (N)

_____. History, Fable and Myth in the Caribbean and Guianas. Georgetown: National History and Arts Council, 1970. [text

of 1970 Edgar Mittelholzer Memorial Lectures] also Caribbean
Quarterly 16, 2 (1970) p. 1 (E)

_____. "Impressions After Seven Years," New World (Fort-
nightly) 44 (1966) p. 17. (E)

_____. "In Memoriam 1948," Kyk-Over-Al 7 (1948) p. 6 (P)

_____. "Interior of the Novel: Amerindian/European/African
Relations," National Identity. Papers Delivered at the Com-
monwealth Literature Conference University of Queensland,
Brisbane, 9-15 August, 1968. ed. K.L. Goodwin. London:
Heinemann, 1970. p. 138 (E)

_____. "Kanaima," p. 142 in Ulli Beier's Black Orpheus.
Ikeja, 1964. also p. 196 Ramchand's West Indian Narrative
also p. 99 Livingston's Caribbean Rhythms also p. 106
Rutherford and Hannah's Commonwealth Short Stories also
p. 112 Thieme's Anthology of West Indian Literature (S)

_____. Kas Kas Interview. Kas Kas: Interviews with Three
Caribbean Writers in Texas. ed. Ian Munro and Reinhard
Sander. Austin, Texas: African and Afro-American Research
Institute of the University of Texas, 1972. (I)

_____. "Kith and Kin," Journal of Commonwealth Literature 7
(1972) p. 1 (A)

_____. "Letter" [to the editor] New World (Monthly)
49 (1966) p. 17 (E)

_____. "The Making of a Book," Georgetown Sunday Chronicle
(15 Oct. 1961). also broadcast BBC 1961 (E)

_____. "The Muse on the Trail," New World (1966) p. 45
[Guyana Independence Issue] (P)

_____. "The Native Phenomenon," Commonwealth. ed. Anna
Rutherford. Aarhus, Denmark: Aarhus University, 1971.
p. 144 (E)

_____. "Orpheus," Kyk-Over-Al 14 (1952) p. 38 (P)

_____. "Other Dimensions," Kyk-Over-Al 14 (1952) p. 39 also
p. 175 Figueroa's Caribbean Voices (P)

_____. Palace of the Peacock. London: Faber, 1960, 1968. (N)

_____. "The Palace of the Peacock," p. 61 Dathorne's Carib-
bean Narrative (N-e)

_____. "Palace of the Stillborn," Kyk-Over-Al 9 (1949)
p. 19 (P)

_____. "The Phenomenal Legacy," Literary Half-Yearly 11, 2
(1970) p. 1 (E)

_____. "The Question of Form and Realism in the West Indian
Artist," Kyk-Over-Al 15 (1952) p. 23 also Harris' Tradition,
The Writer and Society (E)

_____. "Quiet's Event," Kyk-Over-Al 5 (1947) p. 8 (P)

_____. "The Reality of Trespass," Kyk-Over-Al 9 (1949) p. 17 (E)

_____. "Reflection and Vision," Maes-Jelinek's Commonwealth
Literature... (E)

_____. "Rice," Kaie 1 (1965) p. 16 also Poet 13, 1 (1972)
p. 11 (P)

_____. "Savannah Lands," Kyk-Over-Al 2 (1946) p. 8 and 19
(1954) p. 76 (P)

_____. The Secret Ladder. London: Faber, 1963. also in
combined volume with The Whole Armour, London: Faber, 1973. (N)

_____. "The Secret Ladder," p. 69 Dathorne's Caribbean Narra-
tive (N-e)

_____. The Sleepers of Roraima: A Carib Trilogy. London:
Faber, 1970. *Couvade/I, Quiyumucon/Yurokon (S)

_____. "The Spirit of Place," Kyk-Over-Al 17 (1953) p. 228
*The Muse on the Trail/Spirit of the Labyrinth/Spirit of the
Fall/The Golden Age/Laocoon/Creation (P)

_____. "Spirit of the Sea Wall," Kyk-Over-Al 28 (1961)
p. 181 (S)

_____. "Spring Equinox," Kyk-Over-Al 8 (1949) p. 5 (P)

_____. "The Stone of the Sea (Ulysses to Calypso)," Kyk-Over-
Al 22 (1957) p. 24 (P)

_____. "Studies in Realism," Kyk-Over-Al 4 (1947) p. 7 *Vil-
lage in America/The Tragic Muse (P)

_____. "The Sun (Fourteen Poems in a Cycle)," Kyk-Over-Al 20
(1955) p. 175 (P)

_____. Sun Poems I-XIV. [1955 reprint from Kyk-Over-Al] (P)

_____. "Sun Poem XV," Kyk-Over-Al 23 (1958) p. 7 also p. 85
Salkey's Breaklight also New World (1966) p. 54 [Guyana Independence Issue] also p. 99 Seymour's My Lovely Native Land (P)

_____. "A Talk on the Subjective Imagination," New Letters
40, 1 (1973) p. 37 (E)

_____. "Tell Me Trees: What Are You Whispering?" Kyk-Over-Al
1 (1945) p. 10 and 19 (1954) p. 91 also p. 41 Seymour's
Themes of Song also Seymour's Fourteen Guianese Poems for
Children also p. 33 Ramchand and Gray's West Indian Poetry (P)

_____. "These Are the Words of an Old Man," Kyk-Over-Al 19
(1954) p. 117 also p. 48 Seymour's Themes of Song also p. 101
Searwar's Co-Operative Republic also p. 26 Thieme's Anthology
of West Indian Literature (P)

_____. "Tomorrow," Kyk-Over-Al 1 (1945) p. 30 (S)

_____. "Tradition and the West Indian Novel: A Lecture Delivered to the London West Indian Students Union, 15th May 1964," London: West Indian Students Union, 1965. also Harris' Tradition, the Writer and Society also p. 101 Thieme's Anthology of West Indian Literature (E)

_____. Tradition, The Writer and Society. London: New Beacon Publications, 1967. New York: Panther House, 1971. (E)

_____. "Troy," Kaie 4 (1967) p. 73. also Kyk-Over-Al 22 (1957 p. 26. also p. 31 Dathorne's Caribbean Verse also p. 117 Thieme's Anthology of West Indian Literature (P)

_____. Tumatumari. London: Faber, 1968. (N)

_____. "Two Periods in the Work of a West Indian Artist," Kyk-Over-Al 20 (1955) p. 183 [on Denis Williams] (E)

_____. "The Unresolved Constitution," Caribbean Quarterly 14, 1 and 2 (1968) p. 43 (E)

_____. The Waiting Room. London: Faber, 1967. (N)

_____. The Well and the Land (Studies in Time). British Guiana, 1952. *The Well (Prologues of Creation)/The Well (re-creation of the senses)/Charcoal/Agamemnon/Rice (further prologues of creation)/Teiresias (the seer)/Anticleia (the mother) Heracles (the slave)/Achilles (the great runner)/The Glorious Children of the Gods (P)

_____. The Whole Armour. London: Faber, 1962. also in combined volume with The Secret Ladder, London: Faber, 1973. (N)

_____. "Words Written Before Sunset," Kyk-Over-Al 3 (1946) p. 9 (P)

_____. [cf. Seymour, A.J.--"Greatness and Bitterness"]

Hart, Ivry. "Alice Clive," p. 121 Cameron's Guianese Poetry... (P

Hartmann, Stephen J. "Our New Council," Chronicle Christmas Annual (1948) p. 38 (S)

Hartsinck, J.J. Beschryving Van Guiana. Amsterdam, 1770. Vol. I. [transl. by Walter E. Roth as The Story of the Slave Rebellion in Berbice 1762, and publ. in 8 periodical parts-- Nos. 20-27 (Dec. 1958-Sept. 1960) in The Journal of the British Guiana Museum and Zoo and Royal Agricultural Society] (C)

Hawkes, J. "The Bicycle," Chronicle Christmas Annual (1960) p. 33 (S)

Hawkins, Robert. (transl.) *Oho After Death p. 2/Oho Before Hunt p. 1 Poet 13, 1 (1972) [from Wai-Wai poems--excerpt by "T.K."] (P)

Hawley-Bryant, W. "The Song of Guiana's Children," p. 50 Seymour's Themes of Song (P)

Hawtayne, G.H. <u>West Indian Yarns</u>. Georgetown, 1884, 1890. [under pseud. X. Beke] (F)

Hazel, Harrington. <u>The Big Hoax: A Play in Three Acts</u>. [typescript] (D)

_____. <u>Gramps: A Play for Radio in One Act</u>. [typescript] (D)

Heath, Roy. "The Function of Myth," <u>Kaie</u> 8 (1971) p. 19 (E)

_____. <u>Inez Combray</u>. perf. Georgetown: Theatre Guild 1972 (D)

_____. <u>A Man Come Home</u>. London: Longman Caribbean, 1975. (N)

_____. "Miss Mabel's Burial," broadcast Guyana Broadcasting Service 1973 (S)

_____. "Miss Mabel's Funeral," p. 219 Seymour's <u>New Writing in the Caribbean</u> (S)

_____. "The Peasants," <u>Kyk-Over-Al</u> 17 (1953) p. 5 and 19 (1954) p. 116 (P)

_____. "The Wind and the Sun," <u>Savacou</u> 9/10 (1974) p. 55 (S)

<u>Heritage</u>. [ed. Georgetown by Rajkumari Singh and M.R. Monar] (J)

Herrin, Elaine J. <u>Of Flesh and Blood--and God: A Collection of Poems</u>. Guyana, 1972. *My Fish Boy/On Water Street/Young Woman by Bourda/In the Cane Fields/Lunar Deception/The One I Love/The Clouds are Kin to Me/A Greater Love/Koinonia/With Easel and Brush/Of Flesh and Blood-And God/Conflict/Alas! My Humanity/Now Ye Are Clean/Of a Burden/Waiting for Morning/ Morning! (P)

Higgins, Norma. <u>When It Really Matters</u>. broadcast Guyana Broadcasting Service 1975 (D)

Hill, Errol. "Plays of the English-Speaking Caribbean. Part II: Guyana," <u>Bulletin of Black Theatre</u> 3 (1973) p. 11 (Z)

Hillhouse, William. "Expedition up the Cuyuny River, British Guiana, March 1837," <u>Geographical Journal</u>, 1837. (T)

_____. <u>Indian Notices: or Sketches of the Habits, Characters, Languages... of the Several Nations</u> [of British Guiana]. Georgetown, 1820. (C,L)

_____. "Journal of a Voyage up the Massaroony in 1831," <u>Royal Geographical Society Journal</u>, 1831. (A,T)

_____. "Memoir on the Warow Land of British Guiana," <u>Royal Geographical Society Journal</u>, 1834. (A,T)

Hills, Theo L. <u>The Interior of British Guiana and the Myth of El Dorado</u>. 1961. (F,C,T)

Himself Personally. (pseud.) "Jus' Jarge," <u>Christmas Tide</u> (1936) p. 69 (S)

Holder, Iris M. "A Tale Loses Not in the Telling," <u>Chronicle</u> <u>Christmas Annual</u> (1946) p. 3 (S)

_____. "The Tug-O-War," <u>Christmas Tide</u> (1921) p. 31 (S)

Holder, Terence C. "Achievement's Way," <u>Kyk-Over-Al</u> 1 (1945) p. 12 (P)

_____. "The Betrothed," <u>Christmas Tide</u> (1936) p. 81 (S)

_____. "The Way to Life," <u>Christmas Tide</u> (1934) p. 2 (P)

Holder, Wilbert. <u>It's Happening Again: A Play in Two Scenes</u>. [typescript] (D)

Holmes, Cyril. (pseud.?) "Stowaway," <u>Caribia</u> (1946/47) p. 50 (S)

Holzman, Ahouva. "Legend of the Kinnereth," <u>Chronicle Christmas Annual</u> (1946) p. 23 (S)

Homer, Eunice, "The Toiler," <u>Christmas Tide</u> (1949) p. 7 (P)

Hope, Cynthia. "House to Let," <u>Christmas Tide</u> (1936) p. 97 (S)

Hopkinson, Slade. "Azan," <u>Bim</u> 41 (1965) p. 38 (P)

_____. <u>The Blood of a Family: A Play In One Act</u>. perf. Jamaica 1957 (D)

_____. "Don't Hold Your Guilty Griefs...," p. 107 Figueroa's <u>Caribbean Voices</u> (P)

_____. "Electric Eel Song," <u>Bim</u> 43 (1966) p. 186 (P)

_____. <u>Fall of a Chief: A Play in Nine Scenes</u>. perf. Georgetown: Theatre Guild, 1965 (D)

_____. *Ghost p. 95/Going for a Drive p. 93/Lost in a Snowstorm in Connecticut p. 94 <u>Savacou</u> 7/8 (1973) (P)

_____. "Guyana: Freedom Year," p. 74 Figueroa's <u>Caribbean Voices</u> (P)

_____. "In a Certain Garden," <u>Bim</u> 37 (1963) p. 35 (P)

_____. "The Jaguar and the Theorist of Negritude," <u>Bim</u> 44 (1967) p. 274 (P)

_____. "The Madwoman of Papine," <u>Bim</u> 46 (1968) p. 103 also p. 21 Salkey's <u>Breaklight</u> (P)

_____. "The Mighty Intriguer, Calypsonian, Sings His Anticipation of the Coming Carnival," <u>Bim</u> 44 (1967) p. 273 (P)

_____. "Not the Word's Exhibitionist Flight," <u>Bim</u> 41 (1965) p. 37 (P)

_____. "An Oath (for F.H.)," <u>Bim</u> 37 (1963) p. 36 (P)

_____. <u>The Onliest Fisherman; A Play in One Act</u>. Kingston: University of the West Indies, 1967. (D)

_____. "Retour au Pays Natal (For Martin Carter)," <u>Bim</u> 43 (1966) p. 199 (P)

_____. "The Self-Fulfilment of Big Rivers," Bim 42 (1966)
p. 132 also New World (Monthly) 49 (1966) p. 28 also p. 162
Sergeant's Commonwealth Poems of Today (P)

_____. Spawning of Eels. perf. Georgetown 1968 (D)

_____. "The Way Back," Bim 51 (1970) p. 173 (P)

_____. "Worthing: Midnight," Caribbean Quarterly 5, 3 (1958)
p. 168 and 15, 2 and 3 (1969) p. 79 also p. 66 Sergeant's
New Voices of the Commonwealth (P)

Howell, Stella A. "If Never a Christmas," Christmas Tide (1934)
p. 28 (P)

Hoyte, Claude R. "Turn the Other Cheek," Chronicle Christmas
Annual (1951) p. 20 (S)

Hubbard, H.H. "Matchstick La Fargue," Christmas Tide (1936)
p. 45 (S)

Hubbard, Henry Jocelyn Makepeace. "Poor Man's Christmas,"
Demerara Standard (Dec. 1944) (S)

_____. Race and Guyana. Georgetown: author, 1969. (C)

Hudson, William Henry. Green Mansions. 1904. (N)

Hughes, Langston and Arna Bontemps. (eds.) The Poetry of the
Negro, 1746-1949: An Anthology. New York: Doubleday, 1949,
1953. (P)

Humphrey, Hubert H. "The Gloved Hand of Fate," Chronicle Christmas Annual (1959) p. 11 (S)

_____. "The Hidden Voice," Chronicle Christmas Annual (1960)
p. 13 (S)

Humphrey, J.E. "Garuba. A Strolling Player," Kyk-Over-Al 1
(1945) p. 54 (S)

Humphrey, Margaret E. "Legend of Kaiteur," Chronicle Christmas
Annual (1956) p. 21 (P)

Humphrey-Gaskin, Watson A. "Socialists' Psalm," Chronicle Christmas Annual (1951) p. 22 (P)

Hunter, R.B. "Dawn on the Boerasirie," Christmas Tide (1936)
p. 42 (P)

Hutchinson, Doris V. "Bush Rum," Christmas Tide (1949) p. 60 (S)

Hyland, Jacqueline. [cf. Seymour, A.J.--"Standards of Criticism"]

Hylton, Denys. "The Inside Story," Christmas Tide (1950) p. 47 (S)

I

im Thurn, (Sir) Everard F. Among the Indians of Guiana, 1883. (C)

_____. Animism of the Indians of British Guiana, 1880. (C)

_____. Thoughts, Talks and Tramps. London: Oxford, 1934. (M)

Ince, Lucille. "Home for Christmas," Chronicle Christmas Annual
    (1961) p. 25 (S)

An Index to BIM: 1942-1972. comp. by Reinhard W. Sander. St.
    Augustine, Trinidad and Tobago: University of the West Indies,
    1973. (Z)

Ireland, W. Alleyne. (pseud. = Langton) Demerariana--Essays His-
    torical, Critical and Descriptive. Demerara, 1897. (C)

Ishmail, B. Zorina. "And So Goodbye," Chronicle Christmas Annual
    (1958) p. 37 (S)

_____. "Back from the Dead," Chronicle Christmas Annual (1959)
    p. 13 (S)

_____. "Behind the Mask," Chronicle Christmas Annual (1960)
    p. 27 (S)

_____. "The Dead Past," Chronicle Christmas Annual (1958)
    p. 18 (S)

_____. "No Better Gift," Chronicle Christmas Annual (1959)
    p. 19 (S)

Itwaru, Arnold. "At Fort Nassau, Berbice River," Kaie 2 (1966)
    p. 49 (P)

_____. "Burning They Plod," New World (Fortnightly) 38 (1966)
    p. 22 (P)

_____. "Four Themes," Kaie 6 (1970) p. 20   (P)

_____. "In the Woods," Kaie 6 (1970) p. 20 also p. 15 Monar's
    Poems for Guyanese Children (P)

_____. "The River," New World (Fortnightly) 42 (1966) p. 26 (P)

_____. "Voices," New World (Fortnightly) 38 (1966) p. 21 (P)

J

Jack, J.G. "The Yellow Yield," Chronicle Christmas Annual (1948)
    p. 39 (S)

Jagan, Cheddi. "Growing Up," Kaie 4 (1967) p. 25 [extract from
    Jagan's The West On Trial] (A)

_____. "Growing Up On a Sugar Plantation," p. 84 Seymour's
    My Lovely Native Land [extract from Jagan's The West On
    Trial] (A)

_____. The West on Trial. London: Michael Joseph, 1966. (A)

Jahn, Janheinz. A Bibliography of Neo-African Literature from Africa, American and the Caribbean. London: Deutsch, 1965. (Z)

_____. (ed.) Schwarzer Orpheus. Frankfurt: Fisher Bücherei, 1960. (Y)

James, Louis. The Islands in Between. London: Oxford, 1968. (Cr,E)

James, William. "My Excessive Pride," Chronicle Christmas Annual (1959) p. 25 (S)

Jardim, Geoffrey. "Philoso-fee," Expression 2 (1967) p. 12 (P)

Jeffrey, Derrick. "Stand Pipe," Kaie 8 (1971) p. 60 (S)

Jenkins, Valerie T. "Table for Three," Chronicle Christmas Annual (1956) p. 11 (S)

Jenman, G.S. "To Kaieteur (Being an Original and Hitherto Unpublished Diary of a Journey to the Interior of British Guiana)," [extract from Timehri] 1907. (A)

Jeune, Michael. The Cat: A Play for Radio. perf. Guyana 1968 (D)

_____. "The Gambler," broadcast Guyana Broadcasting Service 1974 (S)

John, I.A. "Song of My Soul," p. 171 Cameron's Guianese Poetry... (P)

John-Dorie, Ramdai J. "The Bird," p. 11 Monar's Poems for Guyanese Children (P)

_____. [cf. Ali, Bibi Saffurah Elaine-The New Wave]

Johnson, Clayton. The Broken Egg That Hatched: A Play in the Vernacular in Two Acts. [typescript] (D)

Johnson-Fenty, A. "A Christmas Birthday," Chronicle Christmas Annual (1966) p. 23 (S)

Jones, Verney. "Music at Christmas--Steelband Magic," Kyk-Over-Al 21 (1955) p. 236 also p. 110 Seymour's My Lovely Native Land (C)

Jordan, Oswald D. "When the Prophets Fail," Christmas Tide (1948) p. 40 (S)

Josa, (Rev.) F.P.L. The Apostle of the Indians of Guiana: A Memoir of the Life and Labours of the Rev. W.H. Brett, B.D., for Forty Years a Missionary in British Guiana. London [1888?] (B)

Josiah, Henry W. "And So the Tears," Kyk-Over-Al 19 (1954) p. 92 (P)

_____. "At Takutu," Chronicle Christmas Annual (1966) p. 141 (P)

_____. "Coat-of-Arms for My People," New World (Fortnightly) 40 (1966) p. 7 also p. 113 Searwar's Co-Operative Republic (P

_____. "Girl at the Ferry," Christmas Tide (1949) p. 63 (P)

_____. "Hallelujah Song of the Piaiman," Kaie 6 (1970) p. 25 (P)

_____. "Hindsight of England," Kyk-Over-Al 19 (1954) p. 130 (P)

_____. "How Sam Chase Operates," Kyk-Over-Al 25 (1959) p. 113 (E)

_____. "Kaeituk," broadcast Guyana Broadcasting Service 1973 (S)

_____. "Kankuku Mountains from Lethem," Chronicle Christmas Annual (1966) p. 141 also p. 27 Elma Seymour's Sun is a Shapely Fire (P)

_____. "Know Your Friends," Caribia (1947/48) p. 15 (S)

_____. "Makonaima Returns," Georgetown Daily Chronicle (1966) also p. 75 Robert E. McDowell and Edward Lavitt's Third World Voices for Children. New York: Third Press, 1971, 1972. (S)

_____. "Negro," p. 12 Trotman's Voices of Guyana (P)

_____. "Pork-Knocker's Lament," Caribia (1948/49) p. 57 (P)

_____. "The Short Cut," Chronicle Christmas Annual (1948) p. 26 (S)

_____. "A Sigh," Christmas Tide (1948) p. 5 (P)

_____. "Song of the Wind," p. 65 Elma Seymour's Sun is a Shapely Fire (P)

_____. "They Shall Know Why," Christmas Tide (1950) p. 9 (P)

_____. "Unbroken Silence," Caribia (1950/51) p. 36 (S)

The Journal of Commonwealth Literature. [twice-yearly; began 1966; publishes annual bibliography of Commonwealth litera-ture; articles, interviews, reviews] (J)

K

K., G.D. "By the Way He Acts," Christmas Tide (1935) p. 74 (S)

K., R.H. "A Morning on the Sea Wall," Christmas Tide (1936) p. 41 (P)

Kaie. [began 1965; publ. irregularly; the official organ of the National History and Arts Council of Guyana] (J)

Kanhai, Cyril M. <u>My New Guyana: A Collection of Poems</u>. George-
town: Sheik Sadeek, 1969. *My New Guyana/The Grass-Cutter's
Song/The Symbols/Awake, My Beloved/The Struggle/My Garden/The
Strangest Show in Town/Love Versus Hate/The Selfless One/The
Cane-Cutter's Song/A Prayer for Guyana's Youth/So Let Me
Serve/The New Land (P)

_____. *The New Land p. 24/So Let Me Serve p. 24 <u>Kaie</u> 6
(1970) (P)

_____. "The Struggle," p. 13 Trotman's <u>Voices of Guyana</u> (P)

Kawall, L.M.R. "Sonnet," <u>Christmas Tide</u> (1949) p. 36 (P)

Keane, E.McG. "Seed," <u>Kyk-Over-Al</u> 12 (1951) p. 91 (P)

Kempadoo, Peter. [pseud. = Lauchmonen] <u>Guiana Boy</u>. Crawley,
Sussex: New Literature, 1960. (N)

_____. <u>Old Thom's Harvest</u>. London: Eyre and Spottiswoode,
1965. (N)

_____. "The Rice Cutting Season," p. 88 Seymour's <u>My Lovely
Native Land</u> [excerpt from <u>Guiana Boy</u>] (N-e)

_____. "Rice Money," p. 76 Walmsley's <u>The Sun's Eye</u> [excerpt
from <u>Guiana Boy</u>] (N-e)

Kennedy, Luis. "Roller Chair 99," <u>Christmas Tide</u> (1935) p. 19 (S)

Kesler, C.K. <u>Een Duitsch medicus in Essequebo in de laatse
jaren der 18e eeuw</u>. [A German Medical Doctor in Essequibo
During the Last Years of the 18th Century] 1929. (A)

Khan, Shabir A. "Rain," <u>New World</u> (Fortnightly) 41 (1966) p. 3 (P)

Khan, Yusuf S. <u>Anthology of Political Poems</u>. Guyana: N.G.C.L.
Printers, n.d. *Guyana/Peoples of Guyana/Freedom March/Vote
at Eighteen/Detention/Independence [all by Yusuf S. Khan] (P)

King, Cleo E. "Coloured Women's Call to Action," <u>Chronicle
Christmas Annual</u> (1946) p. 28 (S)

King, Kenneth F.S. "For Me the Sun," <u>Christmas Tide</u> (1949)
p. 15 (P)

King, Paul. *Nausea p. 22/Responsibility p. 22 <u>Expression 2</u>
(1967) (P)

_____. *Not p. 31/In a smug global house I slept... p. 30
<u>Expression 3½</u> (1967) (P)

King, Sheila. <u>Bourdabounty: A Play in Three Acts</u>. [type-
script] (D)

_____. <u>Fo' Betting or Worse: A Two Act Play in the Vernacular</u>.
perf. Georgetown: Theatre Guild 1966 (D)

_____. *Guyana's Rivers p. 27/Majestic Kaieteur p. 26/Mother-
land p. 23/The Road Builders p. 24 Douglas' <u>Guyana Drums</u> (P)

_____. <u>Hands Across the River: A Play in One Act</u>. [typescript] (D)

_____. _A Matter of Policy: A Play in One Act_. [typescript] (D

_____. "Triumph of the Martyrs," p. 14 Trotman's _Voices of Guyana_ (P)

King, Sidney. _Anayug; or, What Everybody Knows; A Modern Parody_. [typescript] (D)

_____. _The Promised Land: A Play in One Act_. perf. Georgetown 1965 (D)

Kirke, Henry. _Twenty-Five Years in British Guiana 1872-1897_. London, 1898. [reprinted Georgetown: Daily Chronicle, 1948. Guiana Edition ed. Vincent Roth] (A)

Kirke, Vernon. _Zorg, A Story of British Guiana_. London: Digby, Long and Co., n.d. (N)

Kissoon, Nasir F.M. "Samuel and the Key to Knowledge," _Kaie_ 10 (1973) p. 40 (S)

Knight, Wilmot. "The Return," _Christmas Tide_ (1935) p. 57 (P)

Knight, Wintle S. "Sunset," _Christmas Tide_ (1934) p. 38 (P)

Kona Waruk. [pseud. cf. Harris, Wilson: _Eternity to Season_ (1952 edn.), and _Fetish_]

Koshland, Miriam. "Poem," _Kyk-Over-Al_ 18 (1954) p. 15 (P)

Kyk-Over-Al. [ed. A.J. Seymour, Georgetown; began 1945; 28 issues up through final no. in 1961] (J)

The Kyk-Over-Al Anthology of West Indian Poetry. [cf. Seymour, A.J.--_Kyk-Over-Al_ 14 (1952) and 22 (1957)]

L

Lab Talk. [publ. monthly, Mackenzie, Linden, Guyana: Guybau] (J)

Laborde, Ernest. "Out of the Shadows," _Kyk-Over-Al_ 13 (1951) p. 206 (P)

Lamazon, Terence. "The Half of All," _Christmas Tide_ (1950) p. 4 (P)

Lambert, Leonard. [cf. Brett, William Henry--_Guiana Legends_]

Lam-Watt, Wanetta. "The Stifling Stillness of Night," _Expression I_ (1966) p. 6 (P)

The Language Forum. [Georgetown: University of Guyana; Vol. 1, no. 1 appeared Aug. 1973] (J)

LaRose, J. Francis Ovren. "No Kindly Face Bent O'er Him," p. 125 Cameron's _Guianese Poetry..._ (P)

_____. Poems of a British Guianese. Georgetown: Persick, 1934. *Manchester/The British West Indies/Guiana, My Own Native Land/A Song of British Guiana/A Welcome to the Assyrians/William Wilberforce/Say, What is This?/Awake, O Afro-Guianese/O Son of Ham/A Red Indian's Soliloquy/The City Life/ Antenuptial Questions/Antenuptial Counsellor/The Brotherhood of Man/Perhaps/The Passing Year/The Coming Year/Two Gossiping Maid Servants/A Drunkard's Pedagogy/A Double Theft/A Belligerent Captain/Death/Far Beyond/If I Had Known/No Kindly Face/ The Twain/Once on A Solitary Day/Her Phantom Friend/She Has Died/Her Last Long Sleep/A Sister's Goodbye/Memorials (P)

LaRose, John. (ed.) New Beacon Reviews. London: New Beacon Books, 1968. (Cr)

Lauchmonen. [pseud. cf. Kempadoo, Peter]

Lawrence, Amy. "Christmas in the 1890's," Kyk-Over-Al 21 (1955) p. 215 also p. 104 Seymour's My Lovely Native Land (A)

Lawrence, Walter MacArthur. "Anticipatory," Kyk-Over-Al 19 (1954) p. 125 (P)

_____. "Call of the Wild," p. 88 Cameron's Guianese Poetry...(P)

_____. "Forward Guiana's Sons," p. 179 Cameron's Guianese Poetry... (P)

_____. "From Meditation, Thoughts in the Silence," Kyk-Over-Al 19 (1954) p. 115 (P)

_____. "Futility," Kyk-Over-Al 19 (1954) p. 114 also p. 47 Seymour's Themes of Song also p. 45 Dathorne's Caribbean Verse (P)

_____. "Kaieteur," Kyk-Over-Al 19 (1954) p. 78 also p. 22 Seymour's Themes of Song also p. 45 Dathorne's Caribbean Verse (P)

_____. Meditation. Thoughts in the Silence. Georgetown, 1933. [philosophical poem consisting of 98 quatrains] (P)

_____. "Morning," Kyk-Over-Al 19 (1954) p. 88 also p. 34 Seymour's Themes of Song (P)

_____. "My Guiana Eldorado," p. 33 A New Guyana (P)

_____. "O Beautiful Guiana," Kyk-Over-Al 19 (1954) p. 64 also p. 11 Seymour's Themes of Song also p. 5 Seymour's Fourteen Guianese Poems for Children (P)

_____. "Ode to Kaieteur," Kyk-Over-Al 2 (1946) p. 6 also p. 81 Cameron's Guianese Poetry... (P)

_____. "Oriens Ex Occidente Lux," Kyk-Over-Al 19 (1954) p. 126 (P)

_____. The Poet of Guiana, Walter Mac A. Lawrence. Selected with a Biography by P.H. Daly. Georgetown: Daily Chronicle, 1948. *Morning Ode/Dawn/Anticipatory?/Inevitable/Threnody/

Unreclaimed/Guiana/Call of the Wild/Moonlight Fantasy/
Kaieteur/The Stream/The Woodlands/A Dream/Our Thoughts/Our
Lives/Our Homes/Royal Requiem/Coronation Ode/Guiana Allegory/
Wisdom Comes/Comparisons/Wide Awake (Rondel)/Yuletide Songs/
Christmas Day (A Rondeau)/Christmas Time (A Rondeau)/Day of
Gladness/Blessed Morn/Vesper (At Sea)/Optional/From Meromi
(Parts II, III, V, VII, Conclusion)/Lorelei (Legendary Siren
of the Rhine)   (P,B)

_____. "The Stars," p. 28 Elma Seymour's _Sun is a Shapely_
Fire (P)

_____. "Sylvan Guiana," p. 84 Cameron's _Guianese Poetry..._ (P)

_____. "Thoughts on Wisdom," _Christmas Tide_ (1936) p. 67 (P)

Lee, Margaret. "A Happy Week-End," _Kyk-Over-Al_ 7 (1948) p. 27 (E)

Leeming, Clifford. (pseud.?) "Back to the Classics," _Caribia_
(1949/50) p. 66 (S)

Lees, Dorothy E. "For Love Came Down," _Christmas Tide_ (1934)
p. 13 (S)

Lefroy, C.E. _Outalissi: A Tale_. 1826. (S)

Leo. [pseud. cf. Martin, Egbert]

Le Queux, William. "The Mystery of 'C.Q.'" _Christmas Tide_ (1923)
p. 2 (S)

Letts, Malcolm. (transl.) _Haus Staden--A True History of His_
Captivity in 1557. London: George Routledge, 1928. (B)

Leubin, Allan. "The Benevolent Prodigal," _Chronicle Christmas_
Annual (1960) p. 35 (S)

Levans, Edward. "Thoughts Removed from Yesterday," _Chronicle_
Christmas Annual (1967) p. 167 (P)

_____. "The United Six," _Chronicle Christmas Annual_ (1966)
p. 93 (P)

Lewis, Alyan. _The Legal Angle: A Play in One Act_. 1963 [type-
script] (D)

_____. _Summer Love: A Play in Four Acts_. 1963. [typescript] (

Liberator. [Archives 1868-1869 incomplete] (X)

A Liburdade. [Archives 1879-1880 incomplete] (X)

Life and Letters (Apr. 1948) and (Nov. 1948) [publ. London:
special West Indian nos.] (J)

Liverpool, A.E. Victor. "Centenary Hymn," p. 170 Cameron's
Guianese Poetry... (P)

Livingston, James T. (ed.) _Caribbean Rhythms. The Emerging_
English Literature of the West Indies. New York: Washington
Square Press, 1974. (Y)

London, Lennox. <u>A Glimpse of the World--Poetry</u>. Georgetown: Labour Advocate Job Printing, n.d. *Poetry/The Realist/The Cynic's Song/The Voice of Yoga/The Wandering Jew/British Guiana/The Ism's/Me/A Lovelorn Lad/Queen Griffone/South African Lament/The Lynching/Free Inequality/The Word of Faith/ African Rallying Song/The Moor in Europe/Benjamin Baniker/The Sky/Caedmon/Lonesome Lennie/Make Me a Cowboy/Episode/The Race/ The Tournament/The Brave Man and the Witch/They Say/Love/Ode to My Love/I First Saw You/If/My Love/My Love (2)/Two Loves/ Defeat/Nurse Badloo/You'll Never Know/My Love for You/Ode to Norma (P)

_____. "Woman of Tigerbay," <u>Kaie</u> 10 (1973) p. 17 (P)

Lowe, Janice "The Bridge," p. 24 Lowe's <u>Expression Six</u> (S)

_____. (ed.) <u>Expression Six</u>. Georgetown, 1970. (Y)

_____. "The Room," <u>Poet</u> 13, 1 (1972) p. 12 also p. 13 Lowe's <u>Expression Six</u> (S)

_____. "Water and Tree," <u>Expression 4</u> (1968) p. 29 (S)

Lowe, Vesta. <u>Guiana Sings</u>. [publ. U.S.?] 1959. (Mu)

Lowhar, O.L. "Archipelago," <u>New World</u> (Fortnightly) 20 (1965) p. 2 (P)

_____. "Barren Peaks," <u>New World</u> (Fortnightly) 23 (1965) p. 4 (P)

_____. "Starflakes," <u>New World</u> (Fortnightly) 6 (1965) p. 27 (P)

_____. "To Martin Carter," <u>New World</u> (Fortnightly) 3 (1964) p. 26 (P)

Luckie, John. "Creole Food," <u>Christmas Tide</u> (1956) p. 25 (S)

Luker, (Rev.) Archibald L. "Guyana National Anthem," <u>Kaie</u> 2 (1966) also Lynette Dolphin's <u>Ten National Songs</u> [The song was entered in a national competition by Luker under the pseud. L.L. Archibald. Luker's revised version was formally approved by the House of Assembly as Guyana's national anthem. Music was composed by R.C.G. Potter] (Mu)

Lupton, S. "A Tragedy of Jazz," <u>Christmas Tide</u> (1923) p. 27 (S)

<u>Lusitano</u>. [Archives 1891 incomplete] (X)

Lynch, Michael A. <u>Mainly Personal</u>. Georgetown, n.d. *Introspection/Retrospection/Orderly Sergeant/Claustrophobia/Blind Beggar/Ruptured Facade/In That Slender Moment/You and Me/To Dorothy/Shadow/Thoughts on the Cliff--or Metaphysics/To John Michael I/To John Michael II/To My Mother/Young Love/Apprehension in a Whiter Vein/Nightmare/Sunday Night/Seven Scenes from a Story of Forbidden Love (P)

Mc

McAndrew, R.C. (ed.) Plexus: A New Magazine of Young Writing. Georgetown, 19-? (Y)

McAndrew, Wordsworth. "Barriat," Kaie 5 (1968) p. 17 also p. 11 Seymour's Magnet (P)

_____. Blue Gaulding. British Guiana , 1958. [Miniature Poet Series] *Blue Gaulding/Wave People/Ignotum/Panacea/ Lobo/Magdalenia/Promenade/Con Fuoco/First Impressions (P)

_____. "Blue Gaulding," Kaie 4 (1967) p. 74 also p. 31 Salkey's Breaklight also p. 56 Elma Seymour's Sun is a Shapely Fire (P)

_____. "First Impression," Kyk-Over-Al 23 (1958) p. 7 (P)

_____. Freedom Street Blues. perf. Guyana 1971 (D)

_____. "Friends," broadcast Guyana Broadcasting Service 1975 (S)

_____. "Guyana--A Cultural Look," p. 117 Searwar's Co-Operative Republic (E)

_____. "Independence," Kaie 2 (1966) p. 44 (P)

_____. "Jollification," Chronicle Christmas Annual (1967) p. 23 (S)

_____. "Last Rites," Kyk-Over-Al 26 (1959) p. 14 (P)

_____. "Legend of the Carrion Crow," Kaie 4 (1967) p. 75 also p. 80 Salkey's Breaklight also p. 58 Seymour's My Lovely Native Land also p. 106 Searwar's Co-Operative Republic (P)

_____. "Legend of the Carrion Crow" [dance interpretation of the poem perf. Georgetown: Theatre Guild in Miss Phoebe] (P,

_____. "Lines to a Cartman Pushing," Chronicle Christmas Annual (1967) p. 76 also Poet 13, 1 (1972) p. 13 also p. 103 Searwar's Co-Operative Republic also p. 9 Seymour's Magnet also p. 10 Thieme's Anthology of West Indian Literature (P)

_____. "Lines to My City from a Rainy Bus," New World 2, 2 (1969) p. 38 (P)

_____. Meditations on a Theme. Georgetown, 1963. (P)

_____. More Poems. Georgetown, 1970. *For Clive Thomas/To a Civil Servant/To Fileen/To Louise/Girl on a Verandah/To My Wife/Massacouraman/To an Unknown Beauty/Lines to My City from a Rainy Bus/Conversation Piece (P)

_____. Ol' Higue. Georgetown: B.G. Litho, 1958. [pamphlet] also p. 4 Monar's Poems for Guyanese Children also p. 107 Searwar's Co-Operative Republic (P)

_____. Poems to St. Agnes. British Guiana, 1962. *Ode/Lines on a Christmas Card, MCMLV/Wind-Bells/Romy/Musica/Lament/Tanka/ Court-Ship/Short-Song/Nexus/Lines Written in the Twenty-first year of my age, when love has drunk me all up/After Being Repulsed/Persistence/Leaving Lines (P)

_____. Selected Poems. Georgetown: Erbar Press, 1966. *Blue Gaulding/Wave People/Con Fuoco/Lines to a Cartman, Pushing/ Amplexus/Magdalenia/To Barbara/Dei Gratia/Legend of the Carrion Crow/Barriat (P)

_____. "Ten Poems in the Japanese Manner," Kyk-Over-Al 24 (1958) p. 50 (P)

_____. Three P's. Georgetown, 1961. [pamphlet] (P)

_____. "To Bibi," p. 8 Seymour's Magnet (P)

_____. "To a Carrion Crow," Kyk-Over-Al 27 (1960) p. 68 (P)

_____. "The Wedding," Chronicle Christmas Annual (1967) p. 96 (P)

McDonald, Hilda. "Dawn," Kyk-Over-Al 11 (1950) p. 38 (P)

_____. "Evensong," Kyk-Over-Al 12 (1951) p. 160 (P)

McDonald, Ian. "Colour-Poem," Jamaica Journal 8, 1 (1974) p. 60 (P)

_____. "Conquistador" ("Hispaniola"), p. 265 Sergeant's Commonwealth Poems of Today (P)

_____. "Death of a Head of State," broadcast Guyana Broadcasting Service 1970 [on Sir David Rose, 1st Governor-General of Guyana] (E)

_____. "Decorated for a Kiss," New World [Guyana Independence Issue] 1966 p. 29 (P)

_____. "The Four Knives of Freeman, the Cane Cutter," Bim 36 (1963) p. 238 also New World (Fortnightly) 42 (1966) p. 22 also Outposts [London] also Best Poems for 1968 [21st Annual vol. of Borestone Mountain Poetry Awards] (P)

_____. "Georgetown Children," p. 19 Seymour's Magnet also in Redvers Brandling's Assembly: Prose and Poems. Macmillan, 1975. (P)

_____. "Green Eyes," Bim 38 (1964) p. 98 (P)

_____. "Hispaniola," Bim 32 (1961) p. 234 (P)

_____. The Humming-Bird Tree. London: Heinemann, 1969, 1975. [Winifred Holtby Prize winner for best regional novel, Royal Society of Literature] (N)

_____. "Jaffo the Calypsonian," Bim 22 (1955). p. 91 also
p. 49 Thieme's Anthology of West Indian Literature also
p. 19 Ramchand and Gray's West Indian Poetry also p. 34
Salkey's Breaklight also Gray's Bite In. Stage 1. also p. 46
Dathorne's Anthology of Caribbean Verse also Compass, New
York: Scott, Foresman, 1971 also Father Anthony DeVerteuil's
Life Lines, Trinidad [publ. by St. Mary's College, Fatima
School, and St. Joseph's Convent] (P)

_____. "Kaiser," Kyk-Over-Al 24 (1958) p. 53 [extract from
The Humming-Bird Tree] (N-e)

_____. "The Law Student," Bim 34 (1962) p. 118 [extract
from novel] (N-e)

_____. "The Legend of Mangamuch and La Cour-Harpe," Bim 31
(1960) p. 163 also New World (Fortnightly) 46 (1966) p. 22 (P)

_____. "Mais of Jamaica," Kyk-Over-Al 28 (1961) p. 186 also
Bim 38 (1964) p. 98 also New World (Fortnightly) 35 (1966)
p. 21 also Gray's Bite In. Stage 1. also Cecil Gray and
Joan Barker's Language for Living; A Caribbean English Course.
Stage 2. London: Longman, 1970. p. 111 (P)

_____. "Mood," Bim 37 (1963) p. 23 (P)

_____. "On An Evening Turned to Rain," Bim 54 (1972) p. 62 (P)

_____. "One Hundred Days to Death," Bim 41 (1965) p. 41 (P)

_____. "Pineapple Woman," Bim 33 (1961) p. 34 also Kyk-Over-
Al 28 (1961) p. 184 also New World (Fortnightly) 33 (1966)
p. 19 also p. 48 Elma Seymour's Sun is a Shapely Fire (P)

_____. "Poem on a Black Stone," Bim 55 (1972) p. 152 (P)

_____. Poems. Georgetown, n.d. [cyclostyled] *Temple Bul-
lock/Rumshop Girl/Young Harpooner/Mood-Lonely Near Educated
Water/Port of Spain Harbour/Bright Cockerel/Decorated for a
Kiss/Mystic at the Nightclub Miramar/Mais of Jamaica/George-
town Children/Son Asleep, Aged Six Months/The Farmer/A White
Man Considers the Situation/Colour Poem/Greeneyes/Indian Love
Statement/Railwaymen/Statement to God/Walking on Lily Leaves/
The Seine Pullers/The Hero/Walking to Sugar Loaf, Antigua/The
Stick Fighters/Jaffo the Calypsonian/Old Moon Rising/Hispaniola/
Pelting Bees/Song in San Fernando/The Weather in Shanty Town/
Pineapple Woman/Poem on a Black Stone/State of the Nation/
Yusman Ali, Charcoal Seller/The Threat to the City/One Hundred
Days to Death/On an Old Woman, Half Gone Mad/The Legend of
Mangamuch and La Cour-Harpe/On an Evening Turned to Rain/
Drunk/The Four Knives of Freeman the Canecutter (P)

_____. Poetry. Introduction 3. London: Faber, 1975. poems
by McDonald in this anthology: *Bright Cockerel/Decorated
for a Kiss/Hispaniola/Indian Love Statement/Mystic at the
Nightclub Miramar/Pelting Bees/Railwaymen/Rumshop Girl/The
Seine Pullers/The Stick Fighters/Yusman Ali, Charcoal Seller (P)

_____. "Poetry in Guyana," Kaie 4 (1967) p. 65 (E)

_____. "Pot O' Rice Horowitz's House of Solace," International Playmen, 1968   (S)

_____. "Railwaymen," Bim 50 (1970) p. 66 (P)

_____. "Rumshop Girl," Bim 51 (1970) p. 134 (P)

_____. "The Seine Pullers," Bim 30 (1960) p. 77 (P)

_____. "Son Asleep--Aged Six Months," Kyk-Over-Al 28 (1961) p. 185 also Bim 41 (1965) p. 28 also p. 81 Sergeant's New Voices of the Commonwealth (P)

_____. "Song in San Fernando," p. 20 Seymour's Magnet (P)

_____. "State of the Nation," Bim 54 (1972) p. 62 also Jamaica Journal 5, 4 (1971) p. 61 (P)

_____. "Statement to God," Bim 41 (1965) p. 43 (P)

_____. "The Stick Fighters," Bim 24 (1957) p. 223 (P)

_____. "Temple Bullock," Bim 37 (1963) p. 22 (P)

_____. "The Threat to the City," Bim 55 (1972) p. 148 also Jamaica Journal 8, 1 (1974) p. 60 (P)

_____. The Tramping Man. perf. Georgetown: Theatre Guild 1969 [also broadcast Guyana Broadcasting Service 1972] (D)

_____. "Trinidadian Love Statement," Bim 32 (1961) p. 234 (P)

_____. "The Unsteady Flame--A Short Account of Guianese Poetry," New World (Fortnightly) 17 (1965) p. 19 = Part I; 18 (1965) p. 24 = Part II; 19 (1965) p. 19 = Part III (E)

_____. "Thoughts for a Guyanese Anthem," New World (Fortnightly) 33 (1966) p. 4 (P)

_____. "Under the Banyan Tree," Penthouse [1972?] (S)

_____. "The Weather in Shanty Town," Bim 52 (1971) p. 226 (P)

_____. "Yusman Ali, Charcoal Seller," Bim 50 (1970) p. 67 also Kaie 8 (1971) p. 34 also Savacou 7/8 (1973) p. 83 [winner of 1970 National Prize for Poetry; awarded A.J. Seymour Poetry Prize 1971] (P)

_____ and Bill Pilgrim, Frank Pilgrim, Ron Robinson, Pauline Thomas, Diane Ng Yen--scriptwriters for Advance to the Brink. perf. Georgetown: Theatre Guild 1969 (D,Mu)

_____. [cf. Seymour, A.J.--"The Literary Tradition in Guyana"]

M'Donnell, A. Considerations on Negro Slavery; with Reports Illustrative of the Actual Conditions of the Negroes in Demarara ... with Suggestions for Ameliorating the Condition of the Slaves, 1824. (C)

McKennie, Ivanhoe. "I Was Dead," Christmas Tide (1949) p. 32 (S)

McKenzie, Claude W. _The Mudlander_. New York: Greenwich, 1966. (N)

Mackenzie Miner. [publ. fortnightly Mackenzie (Linden), Guyana: Demerara Bauxite Co.--continued by _Demba Digest_] (X)

McKetney, Edwin Charles. _Mr. Big_. New York: Pageant Press, 1953. (N?)

McLellan, George H.H. (pseud. = Pugagee Pungcuss) _Old Time Story. Some Old Guianese Yarns Re-Spun._ Georgetown: Daily Chronicle, 1943. [Guiana Edition ed. Vincent Roth--taken from files of _Daily Chronicle_ 1937-38] (F)

McLennan, L.T. "The Progress of Time," p. 161 Cameron's _Guianese Poetry..._ (P)

McMillan, Lorette. (pseud. = Njide) _Points of Departure_. Georgetown, n.d. [untitled poems] (P)

McTurk, Michael. (pseud. = Quow) _Essays and Fables in Verse, Written in the Vernacular of Creoles of British Guiana_. Georgetown: Argosy Office, 1881. [rhymed narratives, written in Creolese] (P,F)

_____. _Essays and Fables--Written in the Vernacular of British Guiana_. A.W.B. Long, 1899. (P,F)

_____. _Essays and Fables in the Vernacular_. Georgetown: Daily Chronicle, 1949. [Guiana Edition ed. Vincent Roth] (P,F)

McWatt, Mark. "Beloved," _Expression_ 3½ (1967) p. 14 (P)

_____. "Curlicues," _Expression 4_ (1968) p. 15 (P)

_____. "Four Songs of the Forest," _Poet_ 13, 1 (1972) p. 14 (P)

_____. *Guyana p. 20/Recital for Doomed Soul p. 27 _Expression I_ (1966) (P)

_____. "Suicide of a Mistress," _Expression 2_ (1967) p. 35 (P)

_____. "What is there, Lilly," _Expression_ 3½ (1967) p. 13 (P)

M

Maes-Jelinek, Hena. (ed.) _Commonwealth Literature and the Modern World_. Brussels: Editions Marcel Didier, 1975. [papers presented at the Conference of Commonwealth Literature at the Univ. of Liège (April 2-5, 1974)] (E)

Makhanlall, David. "Escape from Death," Georgetown _Sunday Chronicle_ (15 Aug. 1971) p. 20 (S)

_____. "It's Cold Everywhere," Georgetown _Sunday Chronicle_ (7 Nov. 1971) p. 8 (S)

_____. "Lottery," Kaie 8 (1971) p. 56 (S)

_____. "Music for a Day," Georgetown Sunday Chronicle (21 Nov. 1971) p. 26 (S)

_____. "A Visit to the Cinema," Kaie 8 (1971) p. 41 (S)

Malcolm, R.S. "Christmas Eve is Dark," Chronicle Christmas Annual (1949) p. 32 (S)

_____. "Once a Year is Plenty," Chronicle Christmas Annual (1950) p. 17 (S)

Mangal, Jaikaran. "An Amerindian's Night of Decision," Kaie 5 (1968) p. 27 (P)

Mann, H. Eileen. *The Crow p. 58/Daybreak and Sunset p. 25/I Laughed a Laugh p. 41/The Silk Cotton Tree p. 67 Elma Seymour's Sun is a Shapely Fire (P)

Manning, Lloyd J. "Barflies," Chronicle Christmas Annual (1957) p. 34 (S)

_____. Cuffy: An Historical Drama in Two Acts. 2nd prize, Republic Month Drama Competition 1970 (D)

_____. The Miracle: A Radio Play. winner Demba Radio Play Competition 1966 (D)

_____. Time and Tide: A Play in Three Acts for Stage and Radio. [typescript] (D)

Martin, A.A.D. [cf. Seymour, A.J.--"Standards of Criticism"]

Martin, Egbert. (pseud.= Leo) "I Can No Longer Hide," Kyk-Over-Al 19 (1954) p. 103 (P)

_____. Leo's Local Lyrics. Georgetown, 1886. *A Shaded Spot/ Serenity/Spirit--Fulness/The Creek/The Bride/The River/The Image/The Forest Walker/The Palm-Soul/The One Power/The Spirit-Stone/The Swallow/The Sorrel-Tree/A Vignette/The Old Book/ Another Vignette/The Present/A Third Vignette/A Patch of Cloud/ Palm Leaves/Vignette the Fourth/The Wraith/The Last Sketch/ Amor/A Dream of Angels/Dost Thou Remember?/Hadst Thou But Spoken!/I Can Remember/I Can No Longer Hide/Lost and Found/ Little Wild Flower/My Darling/Matrimony/Oh! Call It By Some Other Name!/On the River/Oh! Say Not/Patria Mea Te Amo/Regret/ Sing, Bird/Themes of Song/The Two Palms/The Hidden Joy/The Lost Forever/Trade/The Picture/Thine/To Thee/The Locust Tree/ Within Those Depths/Weariness/Writ in Tears/Welcome!/What is the Good (P)

_____. "My Darling," Kyk-Over-Al 19 (1954) p. 103 (P)

_____. "National Anthem," Kyk-Over-Al 19 (1954) p. 131 (P)

_____. *The Poet p. 21/Ruth p. 44/Moonrise p. 62/Sky Pictures p. 67/Calm and Storm p. 68/The Sea p. 71/The River p. 74/The Sorrel Tree p. 82/The Wren p. 83/The Hammock Maker p. 95/On the River p. 105/Absent Friends p. 106/Welcome p. 107/

Additional Lines to National Anthem p. 108/Trade p. 113/The
Negro Village p. 116/The Dog and the Mirror p. 131/The Golden
Milestone Gained p. 146/A Plea for the Children p. 155/To the
Masters p. 156/Looking Back p. 158/For So He Giveth His Be-
loved Sleep p. 167 Cameron's Guianese Poetry... (P)

_____. Poetical Works. London: W.H.L. Collingridge Printers,
1883. *224 pp. of poetry in several sections: Poems/Ruth, A
Poet's Story/The Joys of Night, A Meditation/Silver Chords,
or Heart Poems/Celestial Echoes, or Poems of the Soul/Domestic
Chords, or Narrative Poems (P)

_____. "Resuscitation," Kyk-Over-Al 2 (1946) p. 6 (P)

_____. "The Swallow," Kyk-Over-Al 5 (1947) p. 7 and 19 (1954)
p. 95 also p. 39 Seymour's Themes of Song also p. 55 Elma
Seymour's Sun Is A Shapely Fire also p. 12 Seymour's Fourteen
Guianese Poems for Children also p. 55 Dathorne's Caribbean
Verse (P)

_____. "Themes of Song," Kyk-Over-Al 19 (1954) p. 95 also
p. 11 Seymour's Themes of Song also p. 69 Elma Seymour's Sun
is a Shapely Fire (P)

_____. "Twilight," Kyk-Over-Al 19 (1954) p. 97 also p. 30
Seymour's Themes of Song also p. 7 Seymour's Fourteen Guianese
Poems for Children also p. 56 Dathorne's Caribbean Verse (P)

_____. [cf. Seymour, A.J.--"The Poetry of Egbert Martin"]

Martin, Sidney. 'Enery Swankey: A Tragedy in Three Acts.
British Guiana: F.A. Persick, 19-? (D)

_____. Humour, Sketches, etc. 1916. (M)

_____. Mrs. Farrington's Third Husband. British Guiana,
1916. (D)

Martinborough, G.O. "Across the Mighty Essequibo," Chronicle
Christmas Annual (1954) p. 28 (P)

Martineau, H. "Demerara: A Tale," 1832 (S)

Martins, Nellie. (comp.) List of Books of the Union of Cultural
Clubs of British Guiana in Care and Custody of The Royal Agricultural and Commercial Society of British Guiana. 1962.
[cyclostyled list comp. by the librarian of the Guyana Society
Library] (Z)

Massiah, Claude. "Death," Christmas Tide (1948) p. 9 (P)

Massiah, Keith. "When," Christmas Tide (1949) p. 17 (P)

Matadin, Neville L. *The Cycle p. 15/Pride p. 12/To a Moth p. 20
R.C. McAndrew's Plexus also Kaie 10 (1973) p. 23 (P)

_____. "Environment," Poet 13, 1 (1972), p. 15 also p. 7
R.C. McAndrew's Plexus also Kaie 10 (1973) p. 24 (P)

Matthews, Critchlow. "Tribute to A.J. Seymour," Caribia (1947/
48) p. 71 (P)

Matthews, Marc. *For Cuffee p. 151/Guyana Not Ghana p. 153/
   Portia Faces Life p. 153 Savacou 3/4 (1971) (P)

_____. "Noah," broadcast Guyana Broadcasting Service 1973 (S)

_____. "Poem," New World (Fortnightly) 23 (1965) p. 29 (P)

_____. "Reflections," broadcast Guyana Broadcasting Ser-
   vice (S)

_____. "The Train," broadcast Guyana Broadcasting Service
   1973 (S)

Matthews, Ted Eric. "Creole Remedy," Georgetown Sunday Chronicle (16 Feb. 1969) (S)

_____. "The Letter," Georgetown Sunday Chronicle (13 Sept.
   1970) (S)

Mekdici, Anthony. "The Letter," Chronicle Christmas Annual
   (1953) p. 33 (S)

Melville, (Mrs.) Charles. "The Chain," Chronicle Christmas
   Annual (1953) p. 40 (P)

_____. "A Tiger in the Moonlight," Caribia (1951/52) p. 85 (S)

Melville, Edwina. "In the Night," Kyk-Over-Al 19 (1954) p. 110 (P)

_____. "Poem," Kyk-Over-Al 17 (1953) p. 208 and 19 (1954)
   p. 109 (P)

_____. "Silhouettes," New World (Fortnightly) 17 (1965)
   p. 6 (P)

_____. This is the Rupununi: A Simple Story Book of the
   Savannah Lands of the Rupununi. British Guiana: Government
   Information Service, 1956. (M)

_____. "The Wapishana Indians," p. 74 Seymour's My Lovely
   Native Land (C)

Menkman, W.R. "Essequibosche correspondentie," [Correspondence
   from Essequibo] West-Indische Gids 14 (1932/33) p. 59
   [Amsterdam] (A, Co)

Merriman, Stella E. and Joan Christiani. (comps.) Commonwealth
   Caribbean Writers (A Bibliography). Georgetown: Public Free
   Library, 1970. [Braithwaite, Carew, Harris, Hearne, Lamming,
   Sherlock, Wynter] (Z)

Millar, Vibert A. "White Christmas," Chronicle Christmas Annual
   (1953) p. 21 (S)

Mining Gazette. [Archives 1890-1897 incomplete] (X)

Mirglip, Knarf. [pseud. cf. Pilgrim, Frank]

Mirror. [Georgetown, Sundays, organ of the PPP] (X)

Mitchell, Horace L. "The Glimpses," Christmas Tide (1950)
   p. 30 (P)

_____. "Guiana," Christmas Tide (1949) p. 59 also Kyk-Over-Al 9 (1949) p. 11 (P)

_____. "Night's Kiss," Kyk-Over-Al 7 (1948) p. 5 and 19 (1954 p. 101 also p. 8 Seymour's Fourteen Guianese Poems for Children also p. 32 Seymour's Themes of Song (P)

_____. "Sundown," Kyk-Over-Al 1 (1945) p. 11 (P)

_____. "Sunset Scenes," Kyk-Over-Al 4 (1947) p. 10 (P)

_____. "Tropic Rapture," Kyk-Over-Al 5 (1947) p. 8 (P)

_____. "Water-Wetness," Kyk-Over-Al 6 (1948) p. 6 (P)

Mitchell, William A. *First Love--Broken-Hearted p. 28/Reminiscences of Mazaruni p. 23 Chronicle Christmas Annual (1957) (P)

Mittelholzer, Edgar Austin. The Adding Machine: A Fable for Capitalists and Commercialists. Kingston: Pioneer Press, 1954. (S)

_____. The Aloneness of Mrs. Chatham. London: Library 33, 1965. (N)

_____. "Amiable Mr. Britten," Bim 12 (1950) p. 288 (S)

_____. Before the Curtain Rose. Bim 28 (1959) p. 199 (D)

_____. "Breakdown," Bim 6 (1945) p. 9 (S)

_____. "The Canje," p. 40 Seymour's My Lovely Native Land (C)

_____. "Carnival," Caribia (1946/47) p. 30 (E)

_____. Children of Kaywana. London: Nevill, 1952. New York: Day, 1952. London: Secker and Warburg, 1956, 1960. London: Ace Books, 1959. London: Four Square, 1962. (N)

_____. Children of Kaywana. (translations): Kaywanas Bφrn. transl. Danish by Sonja Rindom. Kφbenhavn: Jesperson og Pio, 1953. Kaywana. transl. German by Georg Goyert and Egon Strohm. Berlin: Blanvalet, 1954. Les Enfants de Kaywana. transl. French by Clément Leclerc. Paris: Là Table Ronde, 1954. I Figli di Kaywana. transl. Italian by Egidio Modena. Milano: Baldini e Castoldi, 1956. De Vrouw Kaywana. transl. Dutch by Hans de Vries. 's-Gravenhage: Zuid-Hollandse Uitgevers-Mij, 1957. (N)

_____. "Children of Kaywana," p. 58 Ramchand's West Indian Narrative (N-e)

_____. The Climate of Eden. [cf. Mittelholzer's Shadows Move Among Them] (D)

_____. Colonial Artist in Wartime: A Poem. British Guiana: [Argosy Co.?] 1941. (P)

_____. "Color, Class and Letters," The Nation 3 (17 Jan. 1959) p. 54 (E)

_____. _Corentyne Thunder_. London: Eyre and Spottiswoode, 1941. New York: Humanities, 1970. London: Heinemann, 1970. (N)

_____. _Creole Chips_. British Guiana: Lutheran Press, 1937. (C)

_____. "The Cruel Fate of Karl and Pierre," _Bim_ 8 (1947) p. 31 (S)

_____. _Eltonsbrody_. London: Secker and Warburg, 1960. (N)

_____. _Entirely Traditional_. 1954 (D)

_____. "Epithalamium," _Caribia_ (1945) p. 94 (P)

_____. _Fears and Mirages_. [typescript] (D)

_____. "For Me--The Backyard," _Kyk-Over-Al_ 3 (1946) p. 8 (P)

_____. "Gerald," _Bim_ 23 (1955) p. 152 (S)

_____. _Ghosts at Their Shoulders_. (D)

_____. _The Harrowing of Hubertus_. London: Secker and Warburg, 1954. New York: Day, 1955 [under title _Hubertus_]. London: Secker and Warburg, 1959 [under title _Kaywana Stock_]. London: Foursquare, 1962. (N)

_____. "Heat in the Jungle," _Bim_ 26 (1958) p. 71 (S)

_____. "Herr Pfangle," _Bim_ 32 (1961) p. 235 (S)

_____. _Hubertus_. [cf. Mittelholzer's _The Harrowing of Hubertus_]

_____. "Hurricane Season," _Bim_ 20 (1954) p. 251 (S)

_____. "In the Beginning--Now--And Then," _Bim_ 13 (1950) p. 75 (P)

_____. "The Intellectual Cissies," _Books and Bookmen_ (Aug. 1962) p. 21 (I)

_____. "Island Tints," p. 182 Figueroa's _Caribbean Voices_ [selections] (P)

_____. "Jasmine and the Angels," _Caribia_ (1946/47) p. 13 (S)

_____. _The Jilkington Drama_. London: Abelard-Schuman, 1965. London: Corgi, 1966. (N)

_____. _Kaywana Blood_. London: Secker and Warburg, 1958. London: Four Square, 1962. New York: Doubleday, 1958 [under title _The Old Blood_]. New York: Crest, Fawcett, World, 1971 [abridged version under title _The Old Blood_]. (N)

_____. _Kaywana Stock_. [cf. Mittelholzer's _The Harrowing of Hubertus_]

_____. _Latticed Echoes: A Novel in the Leitmotiv Manner_. London: Secker and Warburg, 1960. (N)

_____. "Latticed Echoes," _The Tamarack Review_ 14 (1960) p. 59 (N-e)

_____. The Life and Death of Sylvia. London: Secker and Warburg, 1953. New York: Day, 1954. London: Ace Books, 1960. London: Four Square, 1963 [under title Sylvia]. London: New English Library, 1968 [under title Sylvia]. (N)

_____. The Life and Death of Sylvia. (translations): Vie et Mort de Sylvia. transl. French by Jacques and Jean Tournier, Paris: Plon, 1956. Il Sole Nel Sangue. transl. Italian by Giuseppe Gogioso. Milano: A. Rizzoli, 1957. (N)

_____. "Literary Criticism and the Creative Writer," Kyk-Over-Al 15 (1952) p. 19 (E)

_____. Mad Mac Mullochs. London: P. Owen, 1959, 1961. [1st edn. was publ. under pseud. H. Austin Woodsley] London: World Distributors, 1961. (N)

_____. "Manoel's Son," Christmas Tide (1936) p. 90 (S)

_____. "Masquerades," p. 108 Seymour's My Lovely Native Land (A)

_____. "Meditations of a Man Slightly Drunk," Kyk-Over-Al 19 (1954) p. 85. (P)

_____. "Miss Clark is Dying," Bim 5 (1945) p. 24 also p. 211 Salkey's Stories from the Caribbean (S)

_____. "Mr. Jones of Port-of-Spain," Bim 11 (1949) p. 185 (S

_____. A Morning at the Office. London: Hogarth, 1950. New York: Doubleday, 1950 [under title Morning in Trinidad]. London: Heinemann, 1974. (N)

_____. A Morning at the Office. (translations): Un Matin au Bureau. transl. French by Ludmila Savitsky. Paris: Gallimard, 1954. Tempesta a Trinidad. transl. Italian by Bruno Tasso. Milano, 1956. (N)

_____. "A Morning at the Office," p. 13 Salkey's West Indian Stories (N-e)

_____. A Morning in Trinidad. [cf. Mittelholzer's A Morning at the Office]

_____. My Bones and My Flute: A Ghost Story in the Old-Fashioned Manner. London: Secker and Warburg, 1955. London: Corgi, 1958, 1966. London: New English Library, 1974. (N)

_____. "My Bones and My Flute," p. 152 Dathorne's Caribbean Narrative (N-e)

_____. "New Amsterdam," p. 37 Seymour's My Lovely Native Land (C)

_____. No Guileless People. (D)

_____. "October Seventh," Kyk-Over-Al 19 (1954) p. 111 (P)

_____. "Of Casuarinas and Cliffs (an Essay)," Bim 5 (1945) p. 6 (E)

_____. _Of Trees and the Sea_. London: Secker and Warburg, 1956. (N)

_____. _The Old Blood_. [cf. Mittelholzer's _Kaywana Blood_]

_____. "Only a Ghost We'll Need," _Bim_ 17 (1952) p. 8 (S)

_____. _The Piling of Clouds_. London: Putnam, 1961. London: Four Square, 1963. (N)

_____. "Pitch-Walk Mood," _Bim_ 7 (1946) p. 52 (P)

_____. "Portrait with a Background," _Bim_ 18 (1953) p. 93 (S)

_____. "Romantic Promenade: A Divertisment in Minor Chords," _Bim_ 8 (1947) p. 12 (E)

_____. "Samlal," _Bim_ 7 (1949) p. 10 (S)

_____. _The Savannah Years_. [typescript] (D)

_____. _Shadows Move Among Them_. Philadelphia: Lippincott, 1951. London: Nevill, 1952. London: Four Square, 1963. [dramatized as _The Climate of Eden_ by Moss Hart. New York: Random House, 1953. perf. New York, 1953] (N,D)

_____. _Shadows Move Among Them_. (translations): _Glühende Schatten_. transl. German by Egon Strohm. Hamburg: Claasen, 1957. _L' Ombre des Hommes_. transl. French by Claude Vincent. Paris: La Table Ronde, 1953. _La Saga Delle Ombre_. transl. Italian by Aguese Silvestri Giorgi. Milano: Baldini e Castoldi, 1957. _En Welke is Onde Zonde_. transl. Dutch by Max Schuchart. Amsterdam: Em. Querido, 1953. (N)

_____. "The Sibilant and Lost," _Bim_ 13 (1950) p. 2 also _Savacou_ 7/8 (1973) p. 59 [appears in _Bim_ as "Sibiltant and Lost"] (S)

_____. "Something Fishy," _Bim_ 6 (1945) p. 36 (S)

_____. _The Sub-Committee (A Sketch)_. _Bim_ 15 (1951) p. 158 (D)

_____. _A Swarthy Boy_. London: Putnam, 1963. (A)

_____. _Sylvia_. [cf. Mittelholzer's _The Life and Death of Sylvia_]

_____. "Tacama," _Bim_ 9 (1948) p. 2 also p. 76 Salkey's _Caribbean Prose_ (S)

_____. _A Tale of Three Places_. London: Secker and Warburg, 1957. (N)

_____. "A Tale of Three Places," p. 163 Dathorne's _Caribbean Narrative_ (N-e)

_____. _Thunder Returning. A Novel in the Leitmotiv Manner_. London: Secker and Warburg, 1961. (N)

_____. _A Tinkling in the Twilight_. London: Secker and Warburg, 1959. (N)

_____. "Towards Martin's Bay," _Bim_ 21 (1954) p. 10 [excerpt from unpubl. novel] (N-e)

_____. Uncle Paul. London: MacDonald, 1963. New York: Dell, 1965. (N)

_____. "Van Batenburg of Berbice," _Bim_ 19 (1953) p. 172 (E)

_____. "The Virgin," _Kyk-Over-Al_ 19 (1954) p. 116 (P)

_____. The Weather Family. London: Secker and Warburg, 1958. (N)

_____. The Weather Family. (translation: _Hurrikan 'Janet'_. transl. German by Margarete Montgelas. Bremen: Schünemann, 1959. (N)

_____. The Weather in Middenshot. London: Secker and Warburg, 1952. New York: Day, 1953. (N)

_____. The Weather in Middenshot. (translations): _Le Temps qu' il Fait à Middenshot_. transl. French by Jacques and Jean Tornier. Paris: Plon, 1954. _Strani Eventi a Middenshot_. transl. Italian by Silvio Curto. Torino: Ed. Tip. Frassinelli, 1955. (N)

_____. The Weather in Middenshot: A Serio-Comedy. [dramatization of the novel] (D)

_____. "Wedding Day," _Bim_ 14 (1951) p. 78 (S)

_____. "We Know Not Whom to Mourn," _Bim_ 10 (1949) p. 82 also p. 20 Salkey's _West Indian Stories_ also p. 31 Livingston's _Caribbean Rhythms_ also p. 35 Carr's _Caribbean Anthology of Short Stories_ (S)

_____. "West Indian Rights," _Caribia_ (1947/48) p. 25 (S)

_____. With A Carib Eye. London: Secker and Warburg, 1958 (C)

_____. The Wounded and the Worried. London: Putnam, 1962. London: Pan, 1965. (N)

_____. [cf. Seymour, A.J.--"Is There a West Indian Way of Life?"]

_____. Mittelholzer, Edgar Austin. Georgetown: Public Free Library, Government Printery, 1968. [Bibliography of works of Mittelholzer and works on him, with tributes by Martin Carter, William Dow, Daisy Hahnfeld, Edward V. Luckhoo, Lucille Mittelholzer, Arthur J. Seymour. A "Serve Your Country" pamphlet for Guyana Week, 1968] (Z)

Mohamed, Euphema. "Stand Up, Guyana," Georgetown _Sunday Chronicle_ (2 Feb. 1975) p. 9 (P)

Monar, Motilall Rooplall. "Born Free," p. 16 Trotman's _Voices of Guyana_ (P)

_____. "The Cane Cutter," _Chronicle Christmas Annual_ (1966) p. 121 also p. 46 Elma Seymour's _Sun Is A Shapely Fire_ (P)

_____. "The Cemetery," Kaie 6 (1970) p. 27 (P)

_____. *The Cemetery/Creole Gang/The Cowherd/Old Woman/A Vision Brahmdeo Persaud's Poems from Annandale (P)

_____. *The Chimney at Chateau Margot p. 84/Patterns p. 84 Seymour's New Writing in the Caribbean (P)

_____. *The Cowherd p. 29/Creole Gang p. 28/Old Woman p. 30 Kaie 5 (1968) (P)

_____. "De Backoo," p. 12 Monar's Poems for Guyanese Children (P)

_____. *Drought p. 9/Meanings p. 6/Patterns p. 8 Kaie 10 (1973) [under pseud. Eustace Greene] (P)

_____. "Limbo," Heritage 2 (1973) p. 28 (P)

_____. Meanings. Georgetown: author, 1972. *Dreams/Drought/ Monza/The Chimney at Chateau Margot/Going for Lawah/The Brahmin Girl (P)

_____. "Moongaza," Gora Singh's Heritage also p. 8 Monar's Poems for Guyanese Children (P)

_____. *My Song p. 28/They Wake p. 2/To the Dawn p. 27 New World (Fortnightly) 21 (1965) (P)

_____. Patterns. Georgetown: author, 1974. (P)

_____. (comp.) Poems for Guyanese Children. Georgetown: Annandale Writers Group, 1974. (P)

_____. "Veiled Woman," Dawn (1973) (P)

Monize, Henrique. "I Must Go," Chronicle Christmas Annual (1967) p. 22 (P)

Moonasar, George A. Double Trouble. perf. Guyana 1968 (D)

Moore, Harold W.B. *Dark Cloudless Night p. 63/The Dry Season p. 99/A Midnight Rainbow p. 100/The North Wind p. 65/The Sea p. 72 Cameron's Guianese Poetry... (P)

Moore, Robert. Slave Rebellions in Guyana. Georgetown: University of Guyana, 1971. [mimeographed] (C)

Morris, R. *Black Benediction p. 86/For Sale p. 86 Seymour's New Writing in the Caribbean (P)

Morris, R.M. "Gentleman Joe's Gesture," Christmas Tide (1934) p. 42 (S)

Morrison, A. "A Sea Wall Reverie," Christmas Tide (1938) p. 18 (P)

Mortalman, B. "Parallels of Fate," Chronicle Christmas Annual (1966) p. 135 (P)

_____. "Solvency in Rhythm," Chronicle Christmas Annual (1966) p. 75 (P)

Muniram, Hemraj. "A Matter of Circumstance," p. 15 Lowe's
  Expression Six (S)

Munro, Ian and Reinhard Sander. (eds.) Kas-Kas: Interviews with
  Three Caribbean Writers in Texas: George Lamming; C.L.R.
  James; Wilson Harris. Austin, Texas: African and Afro-American
  Research Institute of the University of Texas, 1972. (I)

Munro, Silvia. "A Christmas Wager," Chronicle Christmas Annual
  (1961) p. 28 (S)

Musgrave, George H. "Driftwood," Chronicle Christmas Annual (1953)
  p. 9 (S)

_____. "The Friends of 9282," Chronicle Christmas Annual
  (1952) p. 7 (S)

_____. "9282 (An Apology)," Chronicle Christmas Annual (1951)
  p. 4 (S)

_____. "9282 Celebrates," Chronicle Christmas Annual (1953)
  p. 12 (S)

Muss, J.R. "He Nearly Saw a Ghost," Christmas Tide (1935) p. 55 (S

Muttoo, (Rev.) F.X. Scars of the Cross. New York: Vantage,
  1967. (A)

Muttoo, Henry. "Ah Entitle Foh Me Rights," Heritage 2 (1973)
  p. 2 (P)

N

Naidu, Janet. *A Touch of Loneliness p. 24/Sunshine p. 24 Heritage 2 (1973) (P)

Narine, Clarke S. "The Last Testament," Chronicle Christmas
  Annual (1958) p. 24 (S)

National Library, Georgetown, Guyana. [formerly called Public
  Free Library] Guyanese National Bibliography. [quarterly
  list of books deposited at the National Library, with a
  special author, title, and subject index and a list of Guyanese publishers] (Z)

Neresand, Retep. [pseud. cf. Anderson, Peter]

Netscher, P.M. Histories of the Colonies of Demerary and Berbice. Georgetown. 1888. (C)

New, William. (comp.) Critical Writings on Commonwealth Literatures: A Selective Bibliography to 1970, with a List of Theses
  and Dissertations. University Park: Pennsylvania State University Press, 1975. (Z)

Newark, Paul A. "Whither, Science?" Christmas Tide (1934) p. 28 (P

The New Daily Chronicle. [Archives 1926] (X)

A New Guyana. Georgetown: Ministry of Information, Culture and
    Youth, 1973. [poetry and photographs] (P)

New Nation. Georgetown, Sundays. [official organ of the PNC] (X)

New Nation International. Georgetown, fortnightly. (X)

New World. Georgetown, fortnightly. [vol. 1, no. 1 appeared
    30 Oct. 1964, by New World Associates; final issue was no. 50,
    Jan. 1967; nos. 49 (Dec. 1966) and 50 (Jan. 1967) were labeled
    "Monthly"] (J)

New World Quarterly. [began publ. 1964 by Clive Y. Thomas,
    Georgetown, Guyana; later issues publ. by New World Group,
    Ltd., U.W.I., Mona, Kingston, Jamaica] (J)

Ng Yen, Diane. [cf McDonald, Ian--Advance to the Brink]

Nicole, Christopher. (pseud. = Andrew York and Peter Grange) The
    Amyot Crime. London: Jarrolds, 1965. (N)

_____. Amyot's Cay. London: Jarrolds, 1964. London:
    Cassell, 1974. (N)

_____. Blood Amyot. London: Jarrolds, 1964. London:
    Cassell, 1974. (N)

_____. Dark Noon. London: Jarrolds, 1963. (N)

_____. The Face of Evil. London: Hutchinson, 1971. (N)

_____. King Creole. London: Jarrolds, 1966. [under pseud.
    Peter Grange] (N)

_____. The Longest Pleasure. London: Hutchinson, 1970. (N)

_____. Off-White. London: Jarrolds, 1959. (N)

_____. Operation Destruct. New York: Dell, 1974. (N)

_____. Operation Neptune. New York: Holt, Rinehart and
    Winston, 1972. New York: Dell, 1973. (N)

_____. Ratoon. New York: St. Martin's, 1962. New York:
    Bantam, 1973. (N)

_____. The Self Lovers. London: Heinemann, 1968. (N)

_____. Shadows in the Jungle. London: Jarrolds, 1961. (N)

_____. The Thunder and the Shouting. London: Hutchinson,
    1969, 1970. (N)

_____. The West Indies. London: Hutchinson, 1965. (C)

_____. White Boy. London: Hutchinson, 1966. (N)

Njide. [pseud. cf. McMillan, Loretta]

Nobrega, Cecile E. "The Bargain," Christmas Tide (1950) p. 56 (S)

_____. "Genesis of Stabroek Fantasy," Kyk-Over-Al 25 (1959)
    p. 116 (E)

_____. "The Missing Chisel," Chronicle Christmas Annual (1957) p. 40 (S)

_____. "The Package Marked This Side Up," Chronicle Christmas Annual (1956) p. 7 (S)

_____. "Right to Life," p. 17 Trotman's Voices of Guyana (P)

_____. Soliloquies (In Verse). Georgetown: Master Printery, 1968. *Bronze Woman/My Philosophy/Creed of Guyana/Love/The Search/Truth/Anniversary/Kaleidoscope/Gifts/I Pine/Christmas in the Middle of May/'Twas Summer--Then Winter Came (P)

_____. Stabroek Fantasy: A Musical Extravaganza. perf. Guyana 1956 (D,Mu)

Norsworthy, Michael. [cf. Pilgrim, Frank--On the Brink]

The Nugget. [Archives 1888-1890 incomplete] (X)

O

Obermuller, Prince. "Beggar's Luck," Chronicle Christmas Annual (1953) p. 7 (S)

Ogle, O.C. "The Mark of Cain," Chronicle Christmas Annual (1945) p. 55 (S)

_____. "A Slight Misunderstanding," Chronicle Christmas Annual (1950) p. 46 (S)

_____. "Strategy," Chronicle Christmas Annual (1949) p. 42 (S)

_____. "Unguarded Moment," p. 43 Carr's Caribbean Anthology of Short Stories (S)

O'Grady, William. Princess Marie Minnehaha of Manoa, Guiana. London: Stockwell, 1934. (N)

Oliver, Simon Christian. *Lines. 'Demerara! Farewell' 1840 p. 126/Lines for 1st August, 1838 p. 139 Cameron's Guianese Poetry... (P)

Olton, Steve. "Christmas," Christmas Tide (1934) p. 41 (P)

One Who Knows. (pseud.) "Coincidence," Christmas Tide (1936) p. 74 (S)

Osman, M.A. "Cross of Gold," Chronicle Christmas Annual (1956) p. 32 (S)

_____. "The Kwakwani Incident," Chronicle Christmas Annual (1955) p. 23 (S)

_____. "Not in Doctor Book," Kaie 5 (1968) p. 35 (S)

Oswald, A. It Happened in British Guiana: Stories by an Overseer on a Sugar Estate. Ilfracombe, Devon: Stockwell,
1955. (A,C)

P

P., W.M.E. Abassa: A Play, and Poetical Pieces, Georgetown,
1883. (D,P)

_____. What You Will. Georgetown, 1881. (P)

Pace. (Oct. 1968) [Georgetown: "A Souvenir of Mrs. Gandhi's
Visit to Guyana"] (C)

Palmer, John C. "Call of the Drums," Chronicle Christmas Annual
(1957) p. 12 (S)

The 'Parent,' 1885. "My Infant Boy," p. 164 Cameron's Guianese
Poetry... (P)

Parkinson, William. "Four Old Letters from Guiana," Timehri 13
(1894) (Co)

Parris, John A. "Diamonds are Trumps," Chronicle Christmas
Annual (1956) p. 28 (S)

_____. "Gift Roses," Chronicle Christmas Annual (1954) p. 32 (P)

_____. "The Knave of Hearts," Chronicle Christmas Annual
(1955) p. 17 (S)

Parris, Vernon. "Moonlight at Apoteri," Kyk-Over-Al 19 (1954)
p. 74 (P)

Payne, Hugh Wallston. Towards a Guyanese Culture (An Analysis
of Past Action and Future Needs), Georgetown, 1971. [mimeo-
graphed] (E)

Payne, Tommy. Cinderella's Big Night: A Pageant in One Act.
perf. Guyana 1970 (D)

Peck. [cf. Report of Messrs. Peck and Price...]

The Penny Weekly. [Archives 1869] (X)

Pepperpot. (Guyana) Georgetown. [Bookers Staff Publication] (X)

Pepperpot. (Jamaica) Kingston. (J)

Perry, Ernest. Black Mahogany and Other Poems. Georgetown:
Bovell's Printery, 1971. *This Is My Land/In My Heart/The
New Image/This Is Not Peace/Thoughts Spring Free/I Play With
You/Mother Africa/Black Mahogany (P)

_____. "Dougla," Georgetown Sunday Chronicle (13 Jan. 1973)
p. 13 (P)

_____. Guyana's Child. Georgetown: author, 1973. *Wild Flower-er/Hawkey/Chee-Chee-Chee/Yap!Yap!/Twinky-Linky/Up and Down/The Caribbean/Keys/Carrion Crow/The Mongoose/Mosquito Song/Fisher Woman/The Freedom Band/Calypso/Sour Tamarind/Audrie/Daughter/Ding-Dong-Ding/Traffic March/Cows/The Co-Op Way/Cricket Fun/The Planting Man/Robin/A Farming Guy/Curry/Candle Fly/Bully Buster/Neighbour Janey/Bakes/Birdie/Dawn/Bulldog Rum/Johnny/Coo-co-Doodie Do/Never Trust a Cat (P)

_____. A New Morn. Georgetown: author, 1970. *A New Morn/The Freedom Band/The Banner/The Line is Drawn/Pussy Cat/Troubled Eyes/Big Mouth/Visions of Tomorrow/Epitaph/Just a Dream/True Love/A Farewell to Sir David Rose/In Memory of a Brother/Inconsistency/Reflections/Christmas Fever/Sons of Guyana Arise/Love-Lost Children/In the Domino Pack (P)

_____. "Sad Tidings," Dawn 1, 2 (1971) p. 17 (P)

_____. "Sons of Guyana Arise," p. 16 Monar's Poems for Guyanese Children also p. 57 A New Guyana (P)

Persaud, B. Darendra. Daughter's Dilemma: A Play in Two Acts. 1st prize in British Guiana Theatre Guild Play Writing Competition 1963 (D)

Persaud, Brahmdeo. For the Millions. Georgetown, 1972. *For the Millions/For Vishwani/Whispers/The Cane Cutter/'Beloved'/I am Black/Words of an Indian Immigrant (P)

_____. "For the Millions," p. 13 Monar's Poems for Guyanese Children (P)

_____. "Situations," Kaie 10 (1973) p. 26 (P)

_____. "Whispers," Gora Singh's Heritage (P)

_____ and M.R. Monar and Randall Butisingh. Poems from Annandale. Georgetown: Annandale Writers Group, 1973. *Thoughts/Re-Awakening/For Vishwani/Whispers/Vanity [book has 5 poems by each author] (P)

Persaud, Indar Michael Harry. Poems on Guiana. Georgetown: P.A. Brathwaite, 1965. *Blessed Sir Richard Luyt/Guiana and Guianese/O Burnham of Guiana Sunset!/The Voice of Paradise/Guiana Peace/My Love for Guiana (P)

Persaud, Oma. "After Rain," Kaie 10 (1973) p. 25 (P)

_____. "Seminars," Kaie 8 (1971) p. 31 (P)

Persaud, R.N. Scraps of Prose and Poetry. New Amsterdam: Lutheran Press, 1933. (P,S)

Persaud, W.W. "The Future of British Guiana," Chronicle Christmas Annual (1949) p. 57 (S)

_____. "To India," p. 22 Ramcharitar-Lalla's Anthology of Local Indian Verse (P)

Phillips, Basil A.T. "Sir Cane Cutter," Chronicle Christmas Annual (1945) p. 48 (P)

Phillips, Evan. A Voice from the Trees. Georgetown, 1974.
*Poems = T'ings Bad/Choke An' Rob/Nationalization/Work/Black
Friday/Rice Farmer/The Journey/Going Back/A Constructive Riot/
Mist/The Seawall on Saturday Afternoon/Accra Beach/Church/Fly-
ing/Belief/Accra Beach Revisited/Monty's Crime/Morning After/
Train Ride/When Rufus Dead/Midnight Race/Bush Rum/De Phantom/
At the Cinema/Independence/The Seawall. Stories = Disturbances
and Riots/Love on the Seawall/The Crucifixion (P,S)

Phillips, Fred. Guianese Sherlock Holmes. Demerara Standard
Establishment, 1941. (B)

Phillips, Monica. "The Curtain of the Past," Chronicle Christmas Annual (1946) p. 27 (P)

Pickering, Carlton. The Man Inside. Georgetown: author, 1973. (P)

Piers, Frances Handy. *Creole Speech p. 45/My Homestead p. 69
Chronicle Christmas Annual (1945) (P)

_____. "Dark Horses," Chronicle Christmas Annual (1947)
p. 41 (P)

_____. *Guianese Garden p. 69/I Do Not Know p. 84/Old Sea-
wall p. 69/Victoria Regia p. 69 Kyk-Over-Al 19 (1954) (P)

_____. "The Old Sea Wall," p. 16 Seymour's Themes of Song (P)

_____. Rhapsodies of Verse. Ontario, Canada: Jackson Fraser,
1942. *In Memoriam (To Florence)/Mother/Defence/My Immortal-
ity/The Mists/My Desk/Parallel of Life/Wind Eternal/The Rover/
Commonplace/Halifax in Winter Time/Water Weed/The Moon/Sleep/
Ghost of the Avon/Time/Late Autumn in Nova Scotia/Bermuda/My
Forever/Song of a Stranger/The Old Sea Wall/Little Silver Feet/
Guianese Night/Guianese Garden/Late Moon/I Do Not Know/Victoria
Regia/Recompense/Soliloquy/Inspiration/In Memoriam (To Those
Who Lost Their Lives on the "Lady Hawkins")/Vignettes of the
B.G. Coast/Connie/Miniatures: Goldenrod, Planting, Granite/
War (P)

_____. "Rice," Chronicle Christmas Annual (1946) p. 27 (P)

Pieters, Mavis. Onward Guiana: A Play in Four Acts. type-
script (D)

Pilgrim, Bill. "Salute to Guyana," p. 44 A New Guyana (P)

_____. [cf. McDonald, Ian--Advance to the Brink]

Pilgrim, (Rev.) E.S.M. [cf. Seymour, A.J.--"Is There a West
Indian Way of Life?"]

Pilgrim, Frank. Christmas Reunion: A Thirty Minute Play for
Radio in One Act. 1964 [typescript] (D)

_____. "Drama in Guyana," Kaie 4 (1967) p. 35 (E)

_____. The Homecoming: A Thirty Minute Play for Radio.
broadcast 1964; rebroadcast Guyana Broadcasting Service 1971 (D)

_____. "Inside Brinktop," Kaie 1 (1965) p. 24 (E)

_____. Miriamy. A West Indian Play in Three Acts. George-
town: B.G. Lithographic, 1963. [written 1955; perf. Georgetown: Theatre Guild 1962] (D)

_____. "Miss Trinkle Triumphs," Chronicle Christmas Annual
(1950) p. 13 (S)

_____. Rain Stop Play. broadcast Guyana Broadcasting Service
1973 (D)

_____. Singing Rum: A Thirty Minute Play for Radio. broad-
cast 1963; stage adaptation perf. Georgetown: Theatre Guild
1964 (D)

_____. Skeleton at the Party: A Play in One Act. London:
Dean and Sons, 1954. (D)

_____ and Peter Anderson. So This is the Brink. perf. Georgetown: Theatre Guild 1967 [authors used these pseudonyms:
Knarf Mirglip, Retep Neresand] (D)

_____ and Michael Norsworthy. On the Brink. perf. Georgetown:
Theatre Guild 1964 (D)

_____. [cf. McDonald, Ian--Advance to the Brink]

Pinckard, George. Letters from Guiana. [cf. Pinckard's Notes on
the West Indies below] (C)

_____. Notes on the West Indies: Written During the Expedi-
tion Under the Command of the Late General Ralph Abercromby.
London: Longman, 1806. 3 vols. [ed. by Vincent Roth 1942 in
Guiana Edition Series under title Letters from Guiana] (C)

_____. Notes on the West Indies. Westport, Conn.: Negro
Universities Press, 1970. [reprint of the 1806 edn.] (C)

Pinkerton, Z.A. "The Value of a Foe," Christmas Tide (1935)
p. 25 (P)

Plexus. [cf. McAndrew, R.C., ed.]

Poet. An International Monthly. [ed. Madras, India. Vol. 13,
No. 1 (Jan. 1972) was a "Guyana Number"] (J)

Pollard, C.S. "Collector's Item," Christmas Tide (1949) p. 62 (S)

Pollard, F.J. "In Praise of Paedagogy," p. 157 Cameron's Guianese Poetry... (P)

Polson, Alicia. (pseud.?) "Plantation Pay Day," Caribia (1946/
47) p. 7 (S)

Pope, Jessie. "The Hat Trick," Christmas Tide (1923) p. 17 (S)

O Portuguêz. [Archives 1880-1889 incomplete] (X)

Potter, Gertrude. Road to Destiny. New York: Vantage Press,
1959. (N)

Potter, R.C.G. [cf. Luker, (Rev.) Archibald L.--"Guyana National Anthem"]

Premium, Barton. <u>Eight Years in British Guiana, Being the Journal of a Residence in that Province from 1840-1848, Inclusive.</u> London: Longman, 1850. (A)

Prentiss, Katherine. "The End of the Road," <u>Chronicle Christmas Annual</u> (1946) p. 9 (S)

Price. [cf. <u>Report of Messrs. Peck and Price...</u>]

Prince, Claudius. <u>August Monday Morning</u>. perf. Georgetown: Critchlow Labour College Theatre 1975 (D)

Prince, Ralph. "An Amerindian Tragedy," broadcast Antigua Broadcasting Station 1972 (S)

_____. "Jumbies," <u>Night Vision</u>, 1972. (Linden, Guyana) (E)

_____. "Ol' Higue," <u>Savacou</u> 7/8 (1973) p. 110 (S) ·

_____. "A Plaisance Beauty," <u>The Watookan</u>, 1972. (Linden, Guyana) (P)

_____. "Time, Orange and Philosophy," <u>The Watookan</u>, 1972. (Linden, Guyana) (E)

_____. "The Water Woman and Her Lover," broadcast B.B.C. 1972 (S)

Proctor, Milton. "His Brother's Keeper," <u>Christmas Tide</u> (1934) p. 67 (S)

Psaila, Ivan. "Our New Council," <u>Chronicle Christmas Annual</u> (1948) p. 37 (P)

Puncuss, Pugagee. [pseud. cf. McLellan, George H.H.]

Q

Quail, M.A. "The Fall of Diamond Jack," <u>Chronicle Christmas Annual</u> (1966) p. 20 (S)

Quow. [pseud. cf. McTurk, Michael]

R

R., F. Gordon. "Letter to a Friend," <u>Expression</u> 3½ (1967) p. 33 (P)

R., J. Chronology and Bibliography of Guiana, Printed and Published by James Thomson at his Office, Lot 35, Water Street,
Robbs Town, Georgetown, Demerara, Saturday, September 19th,
1885. [a list of important events, in chronological order,
from 1626 to 1835, with mention of several writings pertain-
ing to Guiana and the Caribbean] (C,Z)

R., V. "The Old Story," p. 97 Cameron's Guianese Poetry... (P)

R., (Mrs.) Z.G. *Great Britain p. 140/The Inundation at Kingston
p. 98 Cameron's Guianese Poetry... (P)

Rain, Thomas. The Life and Labours of John Wray, Pioneer Missionary in British Guiana. London: John Snow, 1892. (B)

Ralegh, (Sir) Walter. The Discoverie of the large, rich, and
beautiful Empire of Guiana, with a relation of the Great and
Golden City of Manoa (which the Spaniards call El Dorado), And
the provinces of Emeria, Arromaia, Amapaia, and other countries, with their rivers, adjoining. Performed in the year
1595, by Sir Walter Ralegh, Knight, Captaine of her Majesties
Guard, Lo. Warden of the Stanneries, and his Highnesse Lieu-
tenant Generall of the Countie of Cornewall. Imprinted at
London by Robert Robinson. 1596. [reprinted numerous times,
the best known reprint being Sir Robert Schomburgk's Hakluyt
Society edn. The Discovery of the Empire of Guyana in 1848;
the use of the word "Discoverie" in Ralegh's title is a dis-
tortion, since he was preceded by other explorers; actually,
Ralegh never ventured into the territory which is today Guyana
proper, but his book is important as one of the earliest commentaries on the general area, and his journey an important
part of the overall history of British expansion in the Amer-
icas] (A,T,C)

Ramchand, Kenneth. (ed.) West Indian Narrative: An Introductory
Anthology. New York: Humanities, 1966. London: Nelson, 1966. (

_____ and Cecil Gray. (eds.) West Indian Poetry: An Anthology
for Schools. Trinidad and London: Longman Caribbean, 1972. (P)

Ramcharitar-Lalla, C.E.J. (ed.) Anthology of Local Indian Verse.
Georgetown: Argosy, 1934. *A Leaky House p. 45/Lips p. 21/
Power and Pride p. 36/The Stars p. 32/The Weeding Gang p. 43 (P

_____. "Christmas at Albion," Chronicle Christmas Annual
(1946) p. 33 (S)

_____. "A Leaky House," p. 15 Seymour's Themes of Song (P)

_____. *A Leaky House p. 86/Lips p. 106/The Stars p. 99/The
Weeding Gang p. 85 Kyk-Over-Al 19 (1954) (P)

_____. "The Weeding Gang," p. 71 Seymour's My Lovely Native
Land also Gora Singh's Heritage also p. 45 Seymour's Themes
of Song (P)

Ramdat, Kuntie K.K. "The Song of the Trade Winds," Kaie 10 (1973)
p. 38 (P)

Ramraj, Victor J. "The Clouds of Christmas," Chronicle Christmas Annual (1959) p. 16 (S)

_____. The Dead Son: A Play in One Scene. perf. Georgetown: Theatre Guild 1966 (D)

Ramsarran, B. Glossary of the Soul. [Georgetown?] *Divine Warning/Why Torture My Word/Immortal Light/Mundane Wealth--Spiritual Poverty/Earth/Oneness/Deck That Man/Poetry/Offering/Which is Real My God/My Burial Bell/My Worldly Tantrum/Eternal Traitors/Run Away Mind/Material Inadequacy/Do Not Expect.../You Are Needed Now/His Highest Honour/Bigots/Freedom/My Wreckage/I Was Born of a Birth Not Unduly Rare/MAHA KALI/Dream No More/The Happiness of Those Days/When I Was Here Some Hours Ago/A Magnificent Absurdity/My Mother, She Dwells on High/The Shopping-Place World/The Highest Price in Sacrifice (P)

Raynor, Leslie. "One Kind of Fool," Chronicle Christmas Annual (1946) p. 41 (S)

_____. "Payment in Kind," Chronicle Christmas Annual (1948) p. 23 (S)

_____. "Swan Song," Chronicle Christmas Annual (1949) p. 25 (S)

The Reflector. [Archives 1889-1892 incomplete] (X)

Reid, Janet. "For My Singing," Christmas Tide (1936) p. 22 (P)

Reis, Eustace H. "Freedom," Christmas Tide (1948) p. 25 (P)

_____. "Garden City of Guiana," Chronicle Christmas Annual (1951) p. 8 (P)

_____. *I Told My Heart p. 102/Poem [Gladness and sorrow, laughter and tears] p. 120/Welcome April p. 89 Kyk-Over-Al 19 (1954) (P)

_____. "Massa Kuraman," Christmas Tide (1934) p. 61 (S)

_____. "Shooting Stars," Christmas Tide (1935) p. 44 (P)

Report of Messrs. Peck and Price, Who Were Appointed at a Meeting of the Free Coloured People of Baltimore, 25th Nov., 1839, Delegates, to Visit British Guiana, and the Island of Trinidad. Baltimore, 1840. (C,T)

Revista/Review Interamericana. [publ. Interamerican Univ. of Puerto Rico, Hato Rey, P.R. Vol. IV, No. 3, 1974, was special Caribbean literature issue] (J)

Richmond, Quentin. "On the Sands of Leguan," Kyk-Over-Al 6 (1948) p. 4 and 19 (1954) p. 15 also Seymour's Fourteen Guianese Poems for Children also p. 14 Elma Seymour's Sun is a Shapely Fire also p. 16 Seymour's Themes of Song (P)

Richmond, Ruby Beldore. "The Fountain of Dreams," Chronicle Christmas Annual (1954) p. 16 (S)

Rickford, Angela E. [cf. Rickford, John R. and Angela E. Rickford--"Masked Africanisms..." below]

Rickford, John. *The Birds p. 9/Limbo p. 25/To a Death p. 23 Expression I (1966) (P)

_____. *The Hole p. 5/It Was a Graduation p. 7/Jilted p. 5/ The Most Audible Silence p. 6 Expression 2 (1967) (P)

_____. "On Steamer Day," Poet 13, 1 (1972) p. 15 (P)

_____. "Pool," Expression 3½ (1967) p. 20 (P)

_____ and Angela E. Rickford. "Masked Africanisms in Guyanese Speech," Georgetown Sunday Chronicle. Part I = 29 Sept. 1974 p. 11; Part II = 6 Oct. 1974, p. 8; Part III = 3 Nov. 1974, p. 8; Part IV = 24 Nov. 1974, p. 7 (L)

Ricknauth, Seenauth. "Lost Love Returned," Chronicle Christmas Annual (1956) p. 39 (S)

Roach, E.M. *The Blind Weavers p. 48/Corn p. 47 Kyk-Over-Al 24 (1958) (P)

_____. "The Old Woman," Kyk-Over-Al 27 (1960) p. 72 (P)

Roberts, Terence. *Approaching Rain p. 22/The Swimmer p. 8 Expression I (1966) (P)

_____. "Finally," Expression 4 (1968) p. 16 (S)

_____. *Ocean p. 6/Regular Passenger p. 7/Street Soul Medley p. 7 Expression 4 (1968) (P)

_____. "For an Unborn Half-Amerindian," Poet 13, 1 (1972) p. 16 (P)

_____. *Going Home p. 21/The Natural Failure p. 22/Pasture p. 19/Stone p. 23 Lowe's Expression Six (P)

_____. "The Interview," Kaie 6 (1970) p. 6 (S)

_____. *I Returned... p. 8/Night p. 9/Steamer Day p. 10 Expression 2 (1967) (P)

_____. *A Lonely Thought p. 11/Poem in 4 Parts p. 7/Scene p. 5/What Happens p. 12 Expression 3½ (1967) (P)

Roberts, William Eaton. "On Kindness," p. 151 Cameron's Guianese Poetry... (P)

_____. Ruins of Time, and Other Poems, 1867. (P)

Robertson, Ian. "Up the Wind Laka Notoo-Boy," p. 73 Giuseppe's Backfire (S)

Robinson, Donald. "Laura," Chronicle Christmas Annual (1957) p. 43 (S)

_____. "Ramona," Chronicle Christmas Annual (1957) p. 19 (S)

_____. "The Roraima," Christmas Tide (1950) p. 9 (S)

Robinson, Donaleen. "Sorrow Hill," <u>Chronicle Christmas Annual</u>
(1958) p. 31 (S)

Robinson, Neville. "Eldorado--To Mervyn Morris," <u>New World</u>
(Fortnightly) 42 (1966) p. 25 (P)

_____. "English Lesson," <u>New World</u> (Fortnightly) 38 (1966)
p. 23 (P)

Robinson, Pat. "The Social Structure of Guyana," p. 51 Searwar's
<u>Co-Operative Republic</u> (E)

Robinson, Ron. [cf. McDonald, Ian--<u>Advance to the Brink</u>]

Rodney, Walter. <u>Groundings with My Brothers</u>. London: Bogle-L'
Ouverture Publications, 1969, 1970. (C)

_____. <u>History of the Upper Guinea Coast</u>. London: Oxford
University Press, 1970. (C)

_____. <u>West Africa and the Atlantic Slave Trade</u>. 1967. (C)

Rodrigues, James C. <u>Poems on Guyana: Verse in Reverie</u>. Georgetown: Forum Printery, 1965. *Guyana/In Our Time/Night Receed-
ing/Independence Call/The Village Lad/My Wife/My Friend/Your
Smile/Love's Prayer/A Pledge/Reverie/The Gambler (P)

Rodrigues, Waveney E. <u>Life's Scrapbook</u>. Ilfracombe, Devon:
Stockwell, 1974. *Dawn/My Soul Unfettered/The Carrion Crow/
A Request/Memory/The Diamond/My Cup of Life/If/What Lies Be-
yond/Contentment/And So Death/Life's Scrapbook/Love's Measure/
Changing Change/A Dedication to Guyana/My Heritage/Uncertainty/
The Search/The Touch/The Soul/Stormy Me/The Average/The Island/
The Stand/The Merger/Equality/Life's Winecup/Soliloquy/Poverty/
Demerara River/The Poor House/To Gypsy/The Grave I Choose/Death/
The Glass Cage/My Son/Toronto's High Park/Toronto/The Reason/
Bind Me Not/Worry/The Key (P)

_____. <u>Reflections: Poems</u>. Southend-on-Sea, Essex: Citizen
Publishing Co., 1962. *O My Dear/Let Me Grow Old/The Grave I
Choose/Come Thou Art Not Unknown/Optimism/A Request/Memory/My
Husband/Silent Lover/My Wish/A Rose/A Prayer/A Mother's Love/
My Prayer/My Son (P)

Rodway, J.A. <u>Guiana, British, Dutch and French</u>. London: T.
Fisher Unwin, 1912. (C)

_____. *Guiana p. 66/The Indians of Guiana p. 72/Kykoveral
p. 68 Seymour's <u>My Lovely Native Land</u> (C)

_____. "Happy Ever After," <u>Christmas Tide</u> (1921) p. 27 (S)

_____. <u>History of British Guiana from the Year 1668 to the
Present Time</u>. Georgetown: J. Thomson, 1891-94. (C)

_____. <u>In Guiana Wilds: A Study of Two Women</u>. London:
Fisher Unwin, 1899. Boston: L.C. Page, 1899. (N?)

_____. <u>The Story of Georgetown</u>. Georgetown: Argosy Co.,
1920. (C)

_____. "Telephone," Kyk-Over-Al 6 (1948) p. 4 and 19 (1954) p. 102 (P)

Rohanie. "Rice Planting," Kaie 8 (1971) p. 29 (P)

Rohlehr, Gordon. "Character and Rebellion in A House for Mr. Biswas," New World Quarterly 4, 4 (1968) p. 66 (E)

_____. "The Creative Writer and West Indian Society," Kaie 11 (1973) p. 48 (E)

_____. "The Historian as Poet," Literary Half-Yearly 11, 2 (1970) p. 171 (E)

_____. "History as Absurdity," Orde Coombs (ed.) Is Massa Day Dead? Black Moods in the Caribbean. Garden City, N.Y.: Anchor, 1974. p. 69 (E)

_____. "Predestination, Frustration and Symbolic Darkness in Naipaul's A House for Mr. Biswas," Caribbean Quarterly 10, 1 (1964) p. 3 (E)

Rohlehr, Lloyd. "Go Away," New World (Fortnightly) 12 (1965) p. 12 (P)

_____. "A Paradise Lost," Chronicle Christmas Annual (1957) p. 9 (S)

_____. "The People," New World (Fortnightly) 6 (1965) p. 17 (P

_____. Thousands Cheer: A Play in Three Acts for Radio. British Guiana, 1960. broadcast 1962 (D)

_____. "The River," Voices (1964) p. 17 (P)

_____. [cf. Seymour, A.J.--"The Arts in Guiana"]

Rooney, Leslie F. "Kijkoveral," Chronicle Christmas Annual (1952 p. 51 (S)

Ross, Evadne. "The Future of British Guiana," Chronicle Christmas Annual (1949) p. 7 (P)

Ross, Hyacinth. Open Confession: A Play in Two Scenes. [typescript] (D)

Roth, Henry D. "How the 'Teur' Came to be Added to the 'Kai'," Chronicle Christmas Annual (1949) p. 4 (S)

Roth, Vincent. "All Aboard for Kurupung: Dream or Prophesy," Chronicle Christmas Annual (1926) (S)

_____. Bibliography of British Guiana Compiled Under the Aegis of the British Guiana Bibliography Committee by its Chairman, Hon. Vincent Roth, M.L.C. by Direction of His Excellency the Governor. 1948. (Z)

_____. *On a Night in Morebo/The Seven Snakes/Story of Atakaleet, the Legend of Kaietuk Chronicle Christmas Annual (1935, 1944) (S)

_____. Pathfinding on the Mazaruni 1922-24. Georgetown: Daily Chronicle, 1949. [Guiana Edition] (A)

_____. "Reminiscences of the Old Demerara," Timehri 4 ser., 1 (32) 1953. p. 28 (A)

_____. Tales of the Trails. Georgetown: Daily Chronicle, 1960. [journal for years 1918-1921] (A)

_____. "A Trip on the Baridi," p. 8 Seymour's My Lovely Native Land (C)

_____. [cf. Bolingbroke, Henry]

_____. [cf. des Voeux, (Sir) William]

_____. [cf. McLellan, George, H.H.]

_____. [cf. McTurk, Michael]

_____. [cf. Pinckard, George]

_____. [cf. St. Clair, (Lt.) Thomas Staunton]

Roth, Walter Edmund. An Inquiry into the Animism and Folklore of the Guiana Indians. New York: Johnson Reprint, 1970. orig. Washington: Bureau of American Ethnology, 1915. (F)

_____. An Introductory Study of the Arts, Crafts and Customs of the Guiana Indians. 38th Annual Report of the Bureau of American Ethnology, 1916-17. (C,F)

_____. "The Little Bush Child," Poet 13, 1 (1972) p. 1 [Amerindian folk tale] (F)

_____. [cf. Hartsinck, J.J.]

_____. [cf. Schomburgk, Richard]

_____. [cf. Van Berkel, Adriaan]

Rowe, Gordon. "Night Flight," Caribia (1945) p. 35 (S)

The Royal Gazette Demarary and Essequibo. [3 times a week; continued Essequibo and Demerary Gazette; Archives 1815-1831 incomplete] (X)

Royal Gazette of British Guiana. [3 times a week; Archives 1831-1889 incomplete] (X)

Ruhoman, Joseph. *Easter p. 31/Nosce te Ipsum p. 34/Ode to Baby Lindbergh p. 19/The South African War p. 39/Threnody p. 27 Ramcharitar-Lalla's Anthology of Local Indian Verse (P)

Ruhoman, Peter. *Bethlehem p. 41/Christmas Morn p. 33/A Christmas Wish p. 30/To the Kiskadee p. 24/A Tropical Morn p. 17/ The Wren p. 26 Ramcharitar-Lalla's Anthology of Local Indian Verse (P)

_____. Centenary History of the East Indians in British Guiana. Georgetown: Daily Chronicle, 1947. (C)

_____. *Kiskadee p. 47/A Tropical Morn p. 35 Kyk-Over-Al 19
(1954) (P)

_____. "To the Kiskadee," p. 37 Seymour's Themes of Song (P)

_____. "Weeding Gang," p. 3 Monar's Poems for Guyanese Child-
ren (P)

_____. "The Wren," p. 57 Elma Seymour's Sun is a Shapely Fire
also Gora Singh's Heritage (P)

Rupan, Dean. "Now, Fallen Light," Expression 3½ (1967) p. 19 (P)

Rutherford, Anna and Donald Hannah. (eds.) Commonwealth Short
Stories. London: Edward Arnold, 1971. (S)

S

Sadeek, Sheik. "Across the Green Fields," Christmas Tide (1949)
p. 57 (S)

_____. Across the Green Fields and Five Other Stories.
Georgetown: Sheik Sadeek, 1974. *Across the Green Fields/The
Sissy/The Magnificent Customer/The Sugar Strike/No Slip-Up!/
Wet and Wild (S)

_____. Black Bush. Georgetown: Sheik Sadeek, 1974. perf.
Georgetown: Critchlow Labour College Theatre 1975 (D)

_____. Black Bush: A One-Shot Radio Play. winner in 1966
Georgetown Demba Play Competition (D)

_____. Bound Coolie; or, the Immigrants: A Play in Three
Acts. 1958 [typescript] (D)

_____. Bundarie Boy. Georgetown: Sheik Sadeek, 1974. [re-
written from the prize-winning manuscript version] (N)

_____. "Candles for My Crib," Caribia (1955) p. 92 (S)

_____. "The Diamond Thieves," Caribia (1949/50) p. 45 (S)

_____. Dreams and Reflections. Georgetown: Sheik Sadeek,
1969. *My Dream/Just/They Came/The Cane Slaves/A Slave's
Prayer/The Canefields/Let Me See/Only Then I'll Sleep/Rice--
Planting Time/'H' (P)

_____. Fish Koker. Georgetown: Sheik Sadeek, 1962. [winner
of Jagan Gold Medal 1961] (D)

_____. Goodbye Corentyne. Georgetown: Sheik Sadeek, 1974.
[written 1965] (D)

_____. He. A Guyanese Play. Georgetown: Sheik Sadeek,
1967. (D)

_____. "Lure of Guyana," <u>Kaie</u> 1 (1965) p. 27 (S)

_____. "The Magnificent Customer," <u>Chronicle Christmas Annual</u> (1967) p. 35 (S)

_____. <u>Namasté</u>. Georgetown: Sheik Sadeek, 1965. 1st prize Georgetown: Theatre Guild Playwriting Competition 1960 also broadcast Radio Demerara 1970 (D)

_____. "No Greater Day," <u>Christmas Tide</u> (1956) p. 15 also <u>Chronicle Christmas Annual</u> (1957) p. 24 (S)

_____. <u>No Greater Day: A Play in One Act</u>. 1965. [typescript] (D)

_____. <u>No Greater Day and Four More Adult Stories</u>. Georgetown: Sheik Sadeek, 1974. *No Greater Day/Ann's Predicament/ The Gulf Between/The Shaft/No More Pavement (S)

_____. "Only Then I'll Sleep," p. 19 <u>A New Guyana</u> (P)

_____. *The Only Man p. 17/Windswept p. 9 <u>Chronicle Christmas Annual</u> (1966) (S)

_____. <u>Pork Knockers</u>. Georgetown: Sheik Sadeek, 1974. [orig. publ. <u>Kyk-Over-Al</u> 25 (1959) p. 148; perf. Georgetown: Theatre Guild] (D)

_____. <u>The Porkknockers and Four Other Stories</u>. Georgetown: Sheik Sadeek, 1974. *The Porkknockers/Beyond the Veil/Fear!!/ No Greater Key/The Five-Cent Ring (S)

_____. <u>Reflections and Dreams and More Poems</u>. Georgetown: Sheik Sadeek, 1974. [enlarged version of the 1969 book, <u>Dreams and Reflections</u>] *A Slave's Prayer/They Came/The Cane Slaves/Just/Men/The Road Gang/My Dream/Let Me See/Rice-Planting Time/The Canefields/Give Me/Only Then I'll Sleep [also, aphoristic "thoughts" interspersed throughout] (P)

_____. <u>Savannah's Edge</u>. Georgetown: Sheik Sadeek, 1968. [written 1965 as adaptation of story "No Greater Day"; perf. Critchlow Labour College Theatre 1975] (D)

_____. "Sugar Canes," p. 246 Seymour's <u>New Writing in the Caribbean</u> (S)

_____. "Sultis, 'Gar and 'The Wits'," <u>Christmas Tide</u> (1950) p. 5 (S)

_____. "The Symphony of Mazaruni," <u>Kyk-Over-Al</u> 12 (1951) p. 133 (C,T)

_____. <u>Windswept</u>. Georgetown: Sheik Sadeek, 1968. *Windswept/Candles for My Crib/Hospitality (S)

_____. <u>Windswept and Other Stories</u>. Georgetown: Sheik Sadeek, 1969. *Windswept/Candles for My Crib/Tomorrow's Sunrise/Lure of Guyana/Black Bush/The Red Blot/Wait 'till Benji Come/Hospitality/Notice to Quit (S)

St. Clair, (Lt.) Thomas Staunton. A Soldier's Sojourn in British Guiana 1806-1808. London: Richard Bentley, 1834. [Guiana Edition ed. Vincent Roth Georgetown: Daily Chronicle, 1947.] (A)

Salkey, Andrew. (ed.) Breaklight: An Anthology of Caribbean Poetry. London: Hamish Hamilton, 1971. (P)

_____. (ed.) Caribbean Prose. London: Evans, 1967. (Y)

_____. Georgetown Journal. A Caribbean Writer's Journey From London Via Port of Spain to Georgetown, Guyana, 1970. Port of Spain, London: New Beacon, 1972. (C)

_____. (ed.) Island Voices: Stories from the West Indies. New York: Liveright, 1970. (S)

_____. (ed.) Stories from the Caribbean: An Anthology. Philadelphia: Dufour, 1965; London: Elek Books, 1965. (S)

_____. (ed.) West Indian Stories. London: Faber, 1960. (S)

Samlallsingh, Ruby. "Sugar Estates Drama Festival," Kyk-Over-Al 25 (1959) p. 125 (E)

_____. [cf. Seymour, A.J.--"Is There a West Indian Way of Life?"]

Sampson, Osbert B. "Cross Roads," Chronicle Christmas Annual (1952) p. 35 (S)

_____. "Thou Canst Not Then Be False," Chronicle Christmas Annual (1951) p. 34 (S)

Sancho, Thomas Anson. Ballad of 1763: The Story of Cuffy's Rebellion Narrated in Verse. Georgetown: author, 1970. (P)

_____. C.L.R. Georgetown, 1972. [on C.L.R. James] (B)

_____. "He," p. 18 Trotman's Voices of Guyana (P)

_____. "The Importance of Our Literature in Caribbean Secondary Education," Kaie 11 (1973) p. 78 (E)

_____. Lines and Rhymes: A Collection of Verse. British Guiana: Labour Advocate Printing Department, 1962. *My Guiana/To S.S./He's Married/Lines Composed on a Good Friend's Quarrel with Me/Three Visions/Sunset Symphony/Our Ancestors/ To My Mother on Having Attained Her Fifty First Birthday/The Awakening/To Zeela/The Everlasting Present/Lines Composed on Good Friday/To Joe/Think Not Our Militance Be Throttled/Gone Forever, Mother Dear/The New Nation/Creole Girl/Elegy on the Death of King George VI/Merci Beaucoup, Mon Cher Ami/Wild Interlude/Christmas/Comrades, Hold On (P)

_____. Spectacles for Drama. 1967. *A Woman's Vengeance/ The Happy Hypocrite [typescript] (D)

_____. Supermen of History. Georgetown: Part I, 1956; Part II, 1957. [includes a chap. on Daly's Story of Guiana's Heroes] (B)

_____. To England and Back. Georgetown: Daily Chronicle, 1967. (C)

_____. "West Indianism," p. 250 Seymour's New Writing in the Caribbean (E)

Sander, Reinhard W. [cf. An Index to BIM]

Sanders, Ivan. "Bank in the Lush," Flamingo (London) 1, 8 (1962) p. 17 (S)

_____. *Her Name was Lola p. 41/Sweepstake Seller p. 4 Caribia (1946/47) (S)

_____. "Tale of a Winter's Night," Caribia (1947/48) p. 12 (S)

Sanders, Ron. "The Adams Family," broadcast Guyana Broadcasting Service 1975 (S)

Saunders, James. Neighbours. perf. Georgetown: Theatre Guild 1969 (D)

Savacou. [publ. quarterly Kingston, Jamaica; began 1970] (J)

Schomburgk, (Von) Richard. Reisen in British Guiana und Oronoko. 1841, 1848. (T,A)

_____. Richard Schomburgk's TRAVELS IN BRITISH GUIANA 1840-1844. Guiana Edition ed. and transl. by Walter E. Roth Georgetown: Daily Chronicle, Vol. I = 1922; Vol. II = 1923. [orig. Leipzig: J.J. Weber] (T,A)

Scoles, Ignatius. Sketches of African and Indian Life in British Guiana. Georgetown: Argosy Press, 1885. (C)

Seaforth, Carol. Big Dilemma: A Play in One Act. 1963. [typescript] (D)

Seaforth, Eardley. *Night in the Village p. 21/On Leave in July 1965 p. 19 Kaie 5 (1968) (P)

_____. "Take a Drink," Poet 13, 1 (1972) p. 17 (P)

Searwar, Lloyd (ed.) Co-Operative Republic. Guyana 1970. A Study of Aspects of Our Way of Life. Georgetown: Government of Guyana, 1970. [essays and poems] (Y)

_____. "The Theatre Guild of British Guiana--1958", Kyk-Over-Al 25 (1959) p. 129 (E)

Seear, A. "Wanted--A Daddy for Christmas," Chronicle Christmas Annual (1955) p. 7 (S)

Seepersaud, Ramdyal. Guiana's People: A Play in the Vernacular in Three Scenes. [typescript] (D)

_____. The Stalwart: A Play in Five Scenes. [typescript] (D)

A Select Bibliography of the Works of Guyanese and on Guyana on the Occasion of Guyana Week, Feb. 19-25, 1967. Georgetown: Government Printery, 1967. [comp. at the Public Free Library] (Z)

Senior, O.E. "Two Chairs at a Desk," Chronicle Christmas Annual (1957) p. 4 (S)

_____. "Watch Those License Plates," Chronicle Christmas Annual (1958) p. 64 (S)

_____. "Young Folks at Home," Chronicle Christmas Annual (1961) p. 30 (S)

Sergeant, Howard. (ed.) Commonwealth Poems of Today. London: John Murray, 1967. [West Indian section pp. 257-271] (P)

_____. (ed.) New Voices of the Commonwealth. London: Evans, 1968. (P)

Seymour, Arthur James. "Against My Old Age," Kyk-Over-Al 8 (1949) p. 5 (P)

_____. "Amalivaca," Kyk-Over-Al 12 (1951) p. 115 = Part I; 26 (1959) p. 1 = Part II; 16 (1953) p. 121 = Part V. [complete version p. 69 Seymour's Selected Poems] (P)

_____. "An einen Calypso-sänger" ("To a Calypso Singer") Jahn's Schwarzer Orpheus, 1954, 1960, 1964. (P)

_____. "Ancient Wisdom," Kyk-Over-Al 16 (1953) p. 123 (P)

_____. "The Arts of Guiana," Kyk-Over-Al 27 (1960) p. 97 [correspondence: Seymour, Allan Young, Mary Woods, Martin Carter, Lloyd Rohlehr, Ken Taharally] (Co)

_____. "As Waters Love the Moon," p. 31 Elma Seymour's Sun Is A Shapely Fire (P)

_____. "Aspen and the American Ethos," Kyk-Over-Al 28 (1961) p. 145 (E)

_____. "Aubade," Kyk-Over-Al 17 (1953) p. 206 (P)

_____. "Autumn in England," Kyk-Over-Al 4 (1947) p. 6 also p. 57 Forde's Talk of the Tamarinds (P)

_____. "Beauty," Christmas Tide (1948) p. 43 (P)

_____. "The Beggars May Have to Become Bandits!: A Modern Anancy Story," Georgetown Sunday Graphic (1 Apr. 1973) p. 4 (S)

_____. A Bethlehem Alleluia. Georgetown, 1974. *The Gates of Day Went Swinging Back/Laid Up Forever in the Fields of Heaven/On Thee, Like Dew at Night, Our Saviour Came/Mary Sings the Infant Jesus Asleep/Breathe With the Whole World's Breath/In Bethlehem a Child (P)

_____. "Beyond," Kyk-Over-Al 6 (1948) p. 8 (P)

_____. Black Song. Georgetown: Labour Advocate, 1971. *Black Song (For Orpheus in Hades)/Practising Scales/For Guy E.L./Steel Band/Image/June the Fourth/Love-Poem/Reality Shyly/Miniatures from Mackenzie/Searching for Our Name/For My Daughters and Sons (P)

_____. "Blind Man's Buff," p. 69 Sergeant's New Voices of the Commonwealth (P)

_____. "Books Out of Doors," Kyk-Over-Al 5 (1947) p. 30 (E)

_____. "Bourda Market," Georgetown Sunday Chronicle (20 Apr. 1975) p. 4 (P)

_____. "Breathe," Kyk-Over-Al 21 (1955) p. 255 (P)

_____. "Buttercup," Kyk-Over-Al 19 (1954) p. 91 (P)

_____. "Caligula," Chronicle Christmas Annual (1936) p. xxiv (P)

_____. Caribbean Literature. British Guiana: F.A. Persick, 1951. [ten 15-minute talks for the Extra-Mural Dept., U.C.W.I., broadcast Radio Station ZFY, British Guiana, 24-26 Sept. 1950] (E)

_____. "Carrion Crows," Chronicle Christmas Annual (1940). p. 29 also Kyk-Over-Al 19 (1954) p. 29 also p. 74 Forde's Talk of the Tamarinds also p. 47 Ramchand and Gray's West Indian Poetry (P)

_____. "Christmas Card," Kyk-Over-Al 21 (1955) p. 255 (P)

_____. "Christmas Gift," Chronicle Christmas Annual (1935) p. 13 [under pseud. Elma Bryce] (S)

_____. "The City in Your Heart," Bim 7 (1946) p. 58 (P)

_____. "City of Memory," Georgetown, 1973. [2 page cover title] (P)

_____. "Common Prayer," Bim 10 (1949) p. 100 also Kaie 3 (1966) p. 29 (P)

_____. "The Continent and the Islands. Open Letter to Roberto Fernandez Retamar (An Anglo-Caribbean Look at Latin American Writers)." Georgetown, 1975. (Cr)

_____. "Contributions of West Indians to Literature: A Lecture Delivered at the Public Library on Friday, 24th January, 1958, at 6 P.M. under the Chairmanship of Anthony Tasker, Esq." British Guiana, 1958. (E)

_____. "The Coronation Ode," Georgetown Daily Chronicle (12 May 1937) p. 16 (P)

_____. "The Creation of Quality in the West Indies," Kyk-Over-Al 18 (1954) p. 43 [1954 Harold Stannard Memorial Lecture] (E)

_____. "Crystal," Kyk-Over-Al 17 (1953) p. 206 (P)

_____. "Cultural Activities, Folklore and Songs," West Indian Review 3, 8 (1958) p. 43 (E)

_____. "Culture in Commonwealth Caribbean Development," p. 100 in David I. Mitchell's With Eyes Wide Open. Bridgetown, Barbados: CADEC, 1973. (E)

_____. "Cultural Values in the Republic of Guyana," p. 79 Searwar's Co-Operative Republic (E)

_____. "Cynic and Eagle," <u>Kyk-Over-Al</u> 11 (1950) p. 61 (P)

_____. <u>Dictionary of Guyanese Folklore</u>. Georgetown: National History and Arts Council, 1975. (C,F,L)

_____. "Divinity," p. 35 Elma Seymour's <u>Sun is a Shapely Fire</u> (P)

_____. "The Earth is a Woman," <u>Kyk-Over-Al</u> 1 (1945) p. 10 (P)

_____. "Easter and the Time of Rice Planting," <u>Kyk-Over-Al</u> 16 (1953) p. 119 (P)

_____. "Edgar Mittelholzer," <u>Kyk-Over-Al</u> 15 (1952) p. 15 (B, Cr)

_____. "Edgar Mittelholzer: Guiana's Swarthy Boy Wrote a Name for Himself." Georgetown <u>Sunday Graphic</u> (9 May 1965) p. 12. (E)

_____. <u>Edgar Mittelholzer, the Man and His Work</u>. Georgetown: The National History and Arts Council, 1968. [text of Edgar Mittelholzer Memorial Lectures delivered 1967] (E)

_____. "Edgar Mittelholzer the Preacher," <u>Kaie</u> 1 (1965) p. 31 (E)

_____. "Edgar Mittelholzer was a Pioneer," Georgetown: Public Free Library. <u>Edgar Mittelholzer 1909-1965</u> (1968) p. xi (E)

_____. "Evening in Hato Rey," <u>New Statements</u> 1, 1 (1971) p. 55 (P)

_____. "Evensong," p. 31 Elma Seymour's <u>Sun is a Shapely Fire</u> (P)

_____. "Exchange of Letters. Standards of Criticism," <u>Kyk-Over-Al</u> 25 (1959) p. 104 (E)

_____. "An Exchange of Letters," <u>Kyk-Over-Al</u> 24 (1958) p. 96 [exchange between Seymour and Denis Williams] (C)

_____. "Festival Call," <u>Official Program, British Guiana Music Festival</u> [later called Guyana Music Festival] for years 1952, 1954, 1956, 1958, 1960, 1964, 1969, 1973. (P)

_____. "Fire and Dew," <u>New Statements</u> 1, 1 (1971) p. 50 (P)

_____. "First of August," <u>Kyk-Over-Al</u> 22 (1957) p. 65 also <u>New Statements</u> 1, 1 (1971) p. 85 also p. 36 Elma Seymour's <u>Sun is a Shapely Fire</u> (P)

_____. "For Christopher Columbus," <u>Kyk-Over-Al</u> 22 (1957) p. 59 also <u>Caribbean Quarterly</u> 5, 3 (1958) p. 187 also p. 8 Gray's <u>Bite In. Stage 3</u>. also p. 74 Figueroa's <u>Caribbean Voices</u> also p. 11 Forde's <u>Talk of the Tamarinds</u> (P)

_____. "For the New Constitution," <u>Kyk-Over-Al</u> 16 (1953) p. 123 also <u>Kaie 2</u> (1966) p. 45 (P)

_____. (ed.) <u>Fourteen Guianese Poems for Children</u>. British Guiana: Master Printery, 1953. (P)

_____. "From Ralegh to Carew. The Books of Guiana," <u>Kyk-Over-Al</u> 27 (1960) p. 74 also publ. Georgetown: Argosy Co., 1960. [P.E.N. Presidential Address, April 1960] (E)

_____. "From the Tower," <u>Kyk-Over-Al</u> 2 (1946) p. 32 ["Literary Look-Out over the Caribbean"] (E)

_____. "Greatness and Bitterness," <u>Kyk-Over-Al</u> 23 (1958) p. 14 [symposium on the concept of the artist: Seymour, Peter Anderson, Martin Carter, Jocelyn D'Oliveira, J.G., Wilson Harris, Frank Thomasson, J.A.E.Y.] (Sy)

_____. <u>Guiana Book</u>. British Guiana: Argosy Co., 1948. *Over Guiana Clouds/Forest Night/The Legend of Kaieteur/Ralegh Comes to Guiana/El Dorado/Kykoveral/There Runs a Dream/Name Poem/Slaves/First of August/Drums/So With a Stride/Just Where it Gurgles/Stabroek Square/Sun Coming Up/The Country House/Men Pruning Trees in Carmichael Street/Evensong on Brickdam Cathedral/Buttercup/Fruit in a Bowl/Sun is a Shapely Fire/For Christopher Columbus/Tomorrow Belongs to the People/To-Morrow (P)

_____. "Guianese History," <u>Kyk-Over-Al</u> 1 (1945) p. 27 (E)

_____. "Guianese Poetry," <u>Kyk-Over-Al</u> 2 (1946) p. 13 (E)

_____. "A Guyanese Poet in Cardiff," [cf. Carter, Martin-- same title]

_____. "History Embedded in the Guyana Novel," <u>Towards Freedom</u> (16 March 1966) [series of broadcasts sponsored by National History and Arts Council for Guyana Independence Celebrations] (E)

_____. "I am the Spirit of the Land," <u>Ours is the Glory</u> p. 3 (P)

_____. <u>I, Anancy</u>. Georgetown: author, 1971. *I, Anancy/ Mango/Fellowship/Crystal/Authority/Portrait of an Old Woman Sleeping/Paradise/Forlorn in Bonafoux/Georgetown Sequences (P)

_____. "I Live in Georgetown," <u>Bim</u> 34 (1962) p. 97 (E)

_____. <u>I Live in Georgetown</u>. Georyetown: author, 1974 (C)

_____. <u>Images Before Easter</u>. Georgetown, 1974. [pamphlet] (P)

_____. "In the Dark, <u>Kyk-Over-Al</u> 11 (1950) p. 15 and 14 (1952) p. 26 (P)

_____. "Introduction," <u>Kyk-Over-Al</u> 25 (1959) p. i [Theatre in British Guiana] (E)

_____. "Introduction to Guyanese Writing," <u>Kaie</u> 7 (1971) p. 4 [series of broadcasts to schools Sept. to Dec. 1971] (E)

_____. "Introduction to the Novel in the British Caribbean," <u>Athenea</u> (N.S.) 1 (March 1964) p. 7 (E)

_____. "An Introduction to the Novels of Edgar Mittelholzer," <u>Kyk-Over-Al</u> 24 (1958) p. 60 (E)

_____. "Introduction to the Poetry of Walter Mac A. Lawrence," Kyk-Over-Al 6 (1948) p. 35 (E)

_____. "Iron Words," Chronicle Christmas Annual (1940) p. 59 (P

_____. "Is There a West Indian Way of Life?" Kyk-Over-Al 20 (1955) p. 188 [symposium: Dr. Frank Williams, H.M.E. Cholmondeley, Martin Carter, Ruby Samlallsingh, P.H. Daly, Edgar Mittelholzer, Rev. E.S.M. Pilgrim] (Sy)

_____. "Issues," Kaie 3 (1966) p. 29 (P)

_____. Italic. Georgetown: author, 1974. *Task/Sugar/Italic/ Self/Sleep/Noughts and Crosses/Mask/Handshake/For Pablo Neruda/ To the Sea/Images Before Easter (P)

_____. "I Was a Boy," p. 44 Elma Seymour's Sun is a Shapely Fire (P)

_____. "The Kaieteur Legend," Chronicle Christmas Annual (1940) p. 22 (P)

_____. (ed.) Kindling of the Flame. Georgetown, 1960. [for the Methodist Bicentenary Celebrations in the Western Area, British Guiana District; includes a hymn = "Thou Infinite Spirit Foreguiding"] (E,Mu)

_____. (ed.) The KYK-OVER-AL Anthology of West Indian Poetry. British Guiana: Argosy Co., 1952. [from Kyk-Over-Al 14 (1952)] (P)

_____. (ed.) The KYK-OVER-AL Anthology of West Indian Poetry. Georgetown: Daily Chronicle, 1957. [from Kyk-Over-Al 22 (1957), a revision of Kyk-Over-Al 14] (P)

_____. Leaves from the Tree. British Guiana: Master Printery, 1951. [Miniature Poet Series] *A New Way/Now All the Winds/ Egypt/Night-Long the Wind/Music I Heard/Honey is Treasure/ Beauty/The Earth is a Woman/Elegy/Requiem for E.L.D./Against My Old Age/Autumn in England/Beyond (P)

_____. "The Legend of Kaieteur," Empire Digest 2, 5 (1945) [Toronto] also p. 96 Thieme's Anthology of West Indian Liter- ature also p. 16 Gray's Bite In. Stage 2 also p. 109 Searwar' Co-Operative Republic also Kyk-Over-Al 19 (1954) p. 81 and 22 (1957) p. 66 also Poet 13, 1 (1972) p. 20 (P)

_____. The Legend of Kaieteur. Georgetown, 1970. [orig. written as narrative poem in 1940; music for the poem com- posed by Philip Pilgrim 1942-44; produced as a "Choral Fantasy" and recorded in Georgetown by George Benson at Queens College 17-18 Feb. 1970] (P,Mu)

_____. "A Letter to John Hearne," Kyk-Over-Al 24 (1958) p. 78 (Cr)

_____. "Letter to Palinurus," Kyk-Over-Al 27 (1960) p. 69 (P)

_____. The Literary Adventure of the West Indies. Kyk-Over-Al 10 (1950). [Seymour wrote this entire issue, with special poetry sections on Jamaica, British Honduras, Antigua, St. Lucia, Barbados, Trinidad, and British Guiana; also sections on historical background, the short story, and the novel] (C,Cr)

_____. "Literature and Caribbean Society," Weekend Post and Sunday Argosy (26 Mar. 1972) p. 11 (E)

_____. A Little Wind of Christmas. Guyana: author, 1967. [broadsheet] (P)

_____. "Long Pants: The Story of a Boy Who Grew Up Overnight," Chronicle Christmas Annual (1937) p. 10 (S)

_____. "Looking at Poetry," Kaie 9 (1973) p. 7 [series of broadcasts to schools Jan.-Mar. 1972 in which Seymour uses for analysis poems by Guyanese writers: Martin Carter, Wilson Harris, J.W. Chinapen, Jan Carew, C.E. Ramcharitar-Lalla, Egbert Martin, Walter Mac A. Lawrence, and A.J. Seymour] (P,Cr)

_____. "Looking at the Venus Statue," Kaie 1 (1965) p. 19 (P)

_____. "Love Song," Kyk-Over-Al 7 (1948) p. 3 (P)

_____. Love Song. Georgetown: author, 1975. [23 untitled "... poems of love written over the years, constituting the Love Song of Arthur Seymour"] (P)

_____. (ed.) Magnet. Georgetown, 1962. includes Seymour's "Dithyramb" and "Thought for Gravesande" (P)

_____. "Main Currents in Caribbean Literature," Commonwealth Journal of the Royal Commonwealth Society. 14, 6 (1970) p. 245 [from a 1968 talk] (E)

_____. [Mais, Roger--a tribute] Kyk-Over-Al 20 (1955) p. 135 (Cr)

_____. "A Marriage Song for Death," Kyk-Over-Al 8 (1949) p. 4 (P)

_____. "Men Pruning Trees," Chronicle Christmas Annual (1941) p. 32 (P)

_____. "Miniatures from Mackenzie," p. 20 Elma Seymour's Sun is a Shapely Fire (P)

_____. "Mirrors," Kyk-Over-Al 16 (1953) p. 124 (P)

_____. Monologue: Nine Poems. Georgetown: author, 1968. *E.R.B.: In Memoriam/Roger Mais/The Three/Othello/Springtide/ Leaf/Christmas Card/River/These Rivers (P)

_____. More Poems. British Guiana: Daily Chronicle, 1940. *Queries/The Last Lover/Dam Giving Way/Easter, 1940/I Cannot Bear/Communication/Sea-Horses/I Dream/Major Movement in A/The Heart Aflame/Fire and Dew/Nocturne in June/The Tree/Strong Heart/Scene/Hymn for Power/To Medusa/West Indian Dance/Pain [When sorrow cases up the speech]/War Calling/Repose/Night-Thoughts/Blind Man's Buff/The Lover Speaks/$20-Note/To the Young Men/Night Crying/Ante-Nuptial (to J.A.E.Y.)/To a Lady Dead/Affirmation (P)

_____. "Morning in the Rupununi," p. 50 Gray's Bite In. Stage 2. also p. 68 Sergeant's New Voices in the Commonwealth also p. 19 Elma Seymour's Sun is a Shapely Fire (P)

_____. "N.E. Cameron (A Profile)," Kyk-Over-Al 26 (1959) p. 50 (B,Cr)

_____. "Nad Guayanov Zamraceno (Uryvky)" ["Over Guyana Clouds"], Vojáka's Černosská, p. 211 (P)

_____. "Name Poem," Kyk-Over-Al 2 (1946) p. 7 and 19 (1954) p. 67 also Kaie 4 (1967) p. 77 and 9 (1973) p. 42 also p. 95 Thieme's Anthology of West Indian Literature (P)

_____. "Nature Poetry in the West Indies, Kyk-Over-Al 11 (1950) p. 39 (E)

_____. (ed.) New Writing in the Caribbean. Georgetown: Guyana Lithographic Co., 1972. *poems by Seymour: Autobio p. 101/The Hand p. 104 (P)

_____. "New Writing in Guyana," Kaie 5 (1968) p. 3 (E)

_____. "Nightly Beside," p. 17 Elma Seymour's Sun is a Shapely Fire (P)

_____. "Not to Be Reconciled (Draft Scene from a Play)," Kyk-Over-Al 15 (1952) p. 58 (D)

_____. "A Note on Literature and Caribbean Society," Kaie 8 (1971) p. 12 (E)

_____. "A Note on Thomas Mann," Kyk-Over-Al 13 (1951) p. 236 (E)

_____. "The Novel in the British Caribbean," Bim 42 (1966) p. 83 = Part I; 43 (1966) p. 176 = Part II; 44 (1967) p. 238 = Part III; 45 (1968) p. 75 = Part IV. (E)

_____. "The Novel in Guyana," Kaie 4 (1967) p. 59 (E)

_____. "The Novel in the West Indies," Kyk-Over-Al 17 (1953) p. 221 (E)

_____. The Novels of Edgar Mittelholzer. British Guiana: Argosy, 1958. [reprinted from Kyk-Over-Al 24 (1958)] (Cr)

_____. "The Novels of Wilson Harris," Bim 38 (1964) p. 139 (E)

_____. One People, One Nation, One Destiny. British Guiana: Ministry of Information, 1959. [broadcast talks] (E)

_____. "Open Letter to West Indian Writers," Kyk-Over-Al 9 (1949) p. 23 (E)

_____. "Over Guiana, Clouds," p. 338 Hughes' The Poetry of the Negro 1746-1949 also p. 178 Galperina's The Time of Flambouy Trees also p. 211 Vojáka's Černosská also p. 40 Figueroa's Caribbean Voices (P)

_____. Over Guiana, Clouds. Georgetown: Demerara Standard Establishment, 1944. *Over Guiana, Clouds/April/Pattern/ Truth/Drink to Me/Perversion/Fertility Poem/First of August/

Grief/Letter to a Friend/For Birth and Death/Dealer in Iron/
Men Pruning Trees/Change/Carrion Crows/Sonnets to Celeste/
Divinity/Song (for Philip Pilgrim)/The Sun Comes Up/Evening
is the Sun/Silence There Is (P)

_____. "Pain" [A screaming hawk pain dives to rake], <u>Kyk-Over-
Al</u> 16 (1953) p. 120 (P)

_____. "A Pair of Spectacles Worn by Abraham Lincoln,"
Georgetown, Guyana: "United States Information Service Bulletin"
for Feb. 1975 (P)

_____. <u>Passport</u>. Georgetown: Labour Advocate Job Printing
Dept., 1972. *Passport/Morocco to Portia/Song/Dialogue/Ances-
tors/I Share/The House/Post Card from Havana/Bogota Nocturne/
On Hearing the Hungarian Quartet at Aspen/My Dream/Issues/To
Hold/Water in Glass/Hand-Song/Lamentito for Rosey Pool/Dirge
for Seferis (P)

_____. <u>Patterns</u>. Georgetown: author, 1970. *Ganga Manni/
Satira Gal/Song for Lulu/I Was a Boy/Nightly Beside/Time/Bitter
Ballad/Poem for Tagore/Looking at the Venus Statue (P)

_____. "Pea Soup," <u>Chronicle Christmas Annual</u> (1939) p. 17 (S)

_____. "A Personal Approach to Poetry," lecture delivered
U.W.I., Cave Hill, Barbados 30 May 1971; also at Guyana National History and Arts Council, 26 July 1971 (E)

_____. "Poem" [Let the wind hurl huge summer] <u>Kyk-Over-Al</u>
17 (1953) p. 207 (P)

_____. "Poem" [Oh light] <u>Kyk-Over-Al</u> 23 (1958) p. 8 (P)

_____. "Poem of Courtship," <u>Kyk-Over-Al</u> 16 (1953) p. 119 (P)

_____. "The Poetical Imagination at Work," <u>Kaie</u> 2 (1966)
p. 28 (E)

_____. "Poetry and Spiritual Values," <u>Kyk-Over-Al</u> 8 (1949)
p. 9 (E)

_____. "Poetry in Guyana," <u>Kaie</u> 4 (1967) p. 64 (E)

_____. "Poetry in These Sunny Lands," <u>Caribia</u> (1945) p. 84 (E)

_____. "The Poetry of Egbert Martin (Leo)," <u>Kyk-Over-Al</u> 3
(1946) p. 19 (E)

_____. "Property Qualifications," <u>Chronicle Christmas Annual</u>
(1938) p. 45 (S)

_____. "Quarter Mile," <u>Chronicle Christmas Annual</u> (1936)
p. 10 (S)

_____. "Der Quell" ["The Well"], Jahn's <u>Schwarzer Orpheus</u>
1954, 1960, 1964 (P)

_____ "Raleigh Comes to Guyana," p. 17 Gray's <u>Bite In. Stage 1</u>. (P)

_____. "Raleigh Proplvje na Guayauv" ["Raleigh Comes to
Guyana"], p. 214 Vojáka's <u>Černošská</u> (P)

99

_____. "Reflections on the Conference," Kaie 3 (1966) p. 7 [on the 1966 Caribbean Writers and Artists Conference] (E)

_____. "Requiem for E.L.D." Kyk-Over-Al 4 (1947) p. 6 (P)

_____. "Salute for Frank Collymore," Savacou 7/8 (1973) p. 26 (P)

_____. "Satira Gal," Kaie 1 (1965) p. 18 (P)

_____. "Scene," p. 60 Figueroa's Caribbean Voices (P)

_____. "Sea Music for Undine," Kyk-Over-Al 9 (1949) p. 20 and 14 (1952) p. 25 (P)

_____. Selected Poems. British Guiana: British Guiana Lithographic Co., 1965. *Legion/Caligula/Blind Man's Buff/Dam Giving Way/Affirmation/I Dream/The Lover Speaks/West Indian Dance/Scene/To a Lady Dead/Repose/Fire and Dew/Over Guiana, Clouds/Kykoveral/Name Poem/First of August/Sun is a Shapely Fire/Evensong/I Dream of Diocletian/Prayer for a Youngster/Songs/Buttercup/Fruit in a Bowl/There Runs a Dream/Stabroek Square/The Legend of Kaieteur/For Christopher Columbus/Always You Guard/Love then a Light/As Waters Love/Night-Long the Wind/Autumn in England/Tomorrow Belongs to the People/The Well/To a Calypso Singer/Ancient Wisdom/Sea Music for Undine/Cynic and Eagle/In the Dark/Egypt/A New Way/Requiem for E.L.D./Amalivaca/Oh Light/To Easter/Variations on a Theme/The Rice Harvest/Evening in Hato Rey/Morning in the Rupununi/In Dark Gethsemane/Who Comes Home/His Grace (P)

_____. Six Songs. Georgetown: author, 1946. (P)

_____. "Song (for Philip Pilgrim)," p. 32 Elma Seymour's Sun is a Shapely Fire (P)

_____. "Song to the Dead Men of Stabroek," p. 12 Elma Seymour' Sun is a Shapely Fire (P)

_____. Song to Man. Georgetown: The Labour Advocate, 1973. *Song to Man/Birthday Dialogue/Rio Night Club/Shirtjac/One Name/For Ronald Lovell/City of Memory/The Best Lack all Convictions/Quiet/Requiem for a Murdered Black/Craft/Death of a Poet/Composition in December/Psalm (P)

_____. "Song of the West Indies," Caribia (1946/47) p. 69 (E)

_____. "Song--While Yet the Dawn," p. 26 Elma Seymour's Sun is a Shapely Fire (P)

_____. "Sonnet for Elaine," Chronicle Christmas Annual (1941) p. 31 (P)

_____. "Sonnets to Elaine" (I and II) Christmas Tide (1938) p. 19 (P)

_____. "Stabroek Square," p. 11 Elma Seymour's Sun is a Shapely Fire (P)

_____. "Standards of Criticism," Kyk-Over-Al 25 (1959) p. 104 [exchange of letters between Seymour, A.A.D. Martin, Frank Thomasson, Richard Allsopp, Jacqueline Hyland, John Gale] (Co)

_____. "The Sun and West Indian Art," Kyk-Over-Al 12 (1951) p. 161 (E)

_____. "Sun is a Shapely Fire," Kyk-Over-Al 14 (1952) p. 23 and 22 (1957) p. 63 also Kaie 4 (1967) p. 76 also p. 9 Elma Seymour's Sun is a Shapely Fire also p. 62 Dathorne's Caribbean Verse also Caribbean Quarterly 5, 3 (1958) p. 185 also p. 82 Salkey's Breaklight [inaccurate version] also p. 170 Livingston's Caribbean Rhythms (P)

_____. "Sunlight and West Indian Poetry," Kyk-Over-Al 4 (1947) p. 17 (E)

_____. Sun's In My Blood. Georgetown: Demerara Standard Establishment, 1945. *Sun is a Shapely Fire/Iron Words/Pupil/ Noah's Dove/Evensong/Beauty is Not Enough/Study in History/I Dream of Diocletian/Song to an Unborn Child/Prayer for a Youngster/Three Songs/Buttercup/Fruit in a Bowl/There Runs a Dream/Stabroek Square/The Legend of Kaieteur/El Dorado/For Christopher Columbus (P)

_____. "Ten Poems," Kyk-Over-Al 16 (1953) p. 119. *Easter and the Time of the Rice Planting/Poem of Courtship/The Well/ Pain/from 'Amalivaca'/To a Calypso Singer/For the New Consti- tution/Ancient Wisdom/With a Great Swirling/Mirrors (P)

_____. Ten Poems. Georgetown: Argosy, 1953. [reprint of Kyk- Over-Al 16 (1953) poems; see previous entry] (P)

_____. (ed.) Themes of Song: An Anthology of Guianese Poetry. Georgetown: B.G. Lithographic, 1961. [includes Seymour's There Runs a Dream/Name Poem/The Legend of Kaieteur/Carrion Crows/Buttercup] (P)

_____. "There Runs a Dream," Kyk-Over-Al 19 (1954) p. 64 also p. 18 Thieme's Anthology of West Indian Literature also p. 58 Gray's Bite In. Stage 3. also p. 164 Sergeant's Commonwealth Poems of Today also p. 39 Ramchand and Gray's West Indian Poetry also p. 40 Walmsley's The Sun's Eye (P)

_____. "Thought for Christmas," Chronicle Christmas Annual (1937) p. 2 (P)

_____. "Three Petals," Kyk-Over-Al 23 (1958) p. 8 (P)

_____. Three Voluntaries. Georgetown: Master Printery, 1953. *Ancient Wisdom/With a Great Swirling/Mind (P)

_____. "Through Other People's Eyes--Experiment in Criticism," Kyk-Over-Al 5 (1947) p. 26 (E)

_____. "The Thursday Poetry Club: A Mosaic," Kyk-Over-Al 26 (1959) p. 13 (E)

_____. "Time's Gate," Chronicle Christmas Annual (~~1938~~) facing p. 17 (P)

_____. "To a Calypso Singer," Kyk-Over-Al 16 (1953) p. 122 also Jahn's Schwarzer Orpheus, p. 132 (1954 edn.), p. 121 (1960 edn.) p. 241 (1964 edn.) (P)

_____. "To Easter," p. 37 Elma Seymour's Sun is a Shapely Fire (P)

_____. "To A Lady Dead," Kyk-Over-Al 14 (1952) p. 24 (P)

_____. "To Medusa," Chronicle Christmas Annual (1938) p. 9 (P)

_____. "Tomorrow," Kyk-Over-Al 5 (1947) p. 12 (P)

_____. "Tomorrow Belongs to the People," Kyk-Over-Al 3 (1946) p. 10 also p. 97 Searwar's Co-Operative Republic (P)

_____. Tomorrow Belongs to the People. El Mañana Pertenece al Pueblo. [Bilingual text; Normal Psaila transl. the 1945 poem into Spanish]. Georgetown, 1975. (P)

_____. (ed.) Twelve West-Indian Poems for Children. Georgetown: Master Printery, 1952. [includes Seymour's "Buttercup"] (

_____. "Two Songs," Bim 11 (1949) p. 251 (P)

_____. Variations on a Theme. Georgetown: Master Printery, 1961. [pamphlet] (P)

_____. Verse. Georgetown: Daily Chronicle, 1937. *Turn These Pages/Salute/Race/Lonely Door/Disintegration/Response/Tears/Joy/Youth's Love Song/Dance/Prayer/A Melody/Baptism/Words/Kaleidoscope/Caligula/Brain-Children/Road/Troilus/Life/The Poet's Song/Caution to Pain/Beauty/Moritura/The Eternal Female/Legion/Resurgence/Jealousy/Dreams/Partnership/Fragments (P)

_____. Water and Blood: A Quincunx. Georgetown: Barrow Printery, 1952. *Easter and the Time of the Rice Planting/Poem of Courtship/The Well/from 'Amalivaca'/Pain (P)

_____. We Do Not Presume to Come...: Seven Poems. Georgetown: author, 1948. *The Gates of Day/On Thee, Like Dew/Breathe with the Whole World's Breath/Mary Had Put Those Hands/And Yet When Love/To Be Divided/Days in a Desert [Hindi language version publ. Lahar, India by Mahendra Kulasrestha, 195?] (P)

_____. "The Well," Kyk-Over-Al 16 (1953) p. 120 also p. 86 Figueroa's Caribbean Voices also Jahn's Schwarzer Orpheus p. 132 (1954 edn.), p. 122 (1960 edn.), p. 240 (1964 edn.) (P)

_____. "The West Indian," Kyk-Over-Al 12 (1951) p. 128 (E)

_____. "West Indian Bookshelf," Kyk-Over-Al 12 (1951) p. 184 (E)

_____. Window on the Caribbean. Georgetown: Persick, 1952. *Historical Sketch/The Economic Bases/Religious Attitudes and

Heritage/Music and Dancing/Art and Architecture/Literature/
The Caribbean World [broadcast Radio Demerara 1952] (E)

_____. "With a Great Swirling," Kyk-Over-Al 16 (1953) p. 124 (P)

_____. "The World Goes On," Chronicle Christmas Annual (1941)
p. 10 (S)

_____. "Xmas Song of the Calvary Tree," St. George's Lance
10, 3 (1959) p. 4 (P)

_____ and Celeste Dolphin. (comps.) The Genius of the Place:
Personal Anthology of Poetry from the British Commonwealth.
Kyk-Over-Al 16 (1953) p. 170 [a British Council Broadcast] (E,P)

_____ and Ian McDonald and Richard Allsopp. The Literary
Tradition in Guyana. Georgetown: The National History and
Arts Council, 1970. (C,Cr)

_____ and Elma Seymour. (eds.) My Lovely Native Land. London
and Trinidad: Longman Caribbean, 1971. Poems by A.J. Seymour
in this anthology: *Name Poem p. 2/There Runs a Dream p. 5/
Kykoveral p. 17/Over Guiana, Clouds p. 31/Carrion Crows p.57/
Bauxite Trains p. 70/Sun is a Shapely Fire p. 100/The Legend
of Kaieteur p. 123. Prose: I Live in Georgetown p. 25/The
Story of Amalivaca p. 117 (Y)

Seymour, Elma. (ed.) Sun is a Shapely Fire. Georgetown: Labour
Advocate, 1973 (P)

_____. [cf. Seymour, A.J. and Elma Seymour--My Lovely Native
Land]

Shahoud, Michael B. "No Silver Lining Ahead," Kaie 8 (1971)
p. 82 (S)

Shepherd, Phyllis and staff of Public Free Library. (comps.)
Guyanese Plays and Their Location (A Bibliography). Georgetown: Public Free Library, 1967. (Z)

Shipp, John P. "Then and Now," Chronicle Christmas Annual (1950)
p. 9 (S)

Simmons, C.D. "O Mighty Kaieteur," p. 80 Cameron's Guianese
Poetry... (P)

Simon, Rick. "The Chinese Soul Box," Chronicle Christmas Annual
(1961) p. 13 (S)

_____. "The Tramp," Chronicle Christmas Annual (1960) p. 39 (S)

Simone, R.C. "Deep River," Chronicle Christmas Annual (1953)
p. 30 (S)

Simone, Ricardo. *The Sea Gull p. 48/The City of Sin p. 91
Kyk-Over-Al 19 (1954) (P)

Singh, Gora. (ed.) Heritage. Georgetown: author, 1973. [program
commemorating 135th anniversary of Indian migration to Guyana:
5th May 1838 - May 1973] (P)

Singh, James J. "The Ghost," <u>Chronicle Christmas Annual</u> (1950)
p. 64 (S)

Singh, Karan B. "Revelation," <u>Chronicle Christmas Annual</u> (1967)
p. 13 (S)

Singh, Krish. <u>It Pays to Buy Local</u>. broadcast Radio Demerara
1975 (D)

Singh, Paul G. "That Angry Wave," <u>Chronicle Christmas Annual</u>
(1953) p. 45 (S)

Singh, R. Lal. <u>A Collection of Poems Celebrating the Richness
of Life</u>. U.S.A.: Gwen Singh, 1971. *Balgobin/Come Light this
Lamp/The Bulbul and the Dhobie Man/The Gem Cutter's Dream/When
We Were Wed/For Gwendolyn and Me/Candle Light/Escape/The Seek-
er of Truth/The Boughs of Love/Karma of the Seasons/The Cricket
King and Queen/Fireside Thought/My Caribee/Her Rainbow Tree/I
Heard a Whisper/Susie/The Thrum of Life (P)

Singh, Rajkumari. "Christmas Story," broadcast Guyana Broadcasting Service 1974 (S)

_____. <u>Collection of Poems</u>. Georgetown: author, 1971. [30
pages of untitled poems] (P)

_____. (ed.) <u>Days of the Sahib</u>. Georgetown, 1971. (P)

_____. "Days of the Sahib," p. 20 Trotman's <u>Voices of Guyana</u> (P

_____. "Epilogue. Karma and the Kaieteur," <u>Kaie</u> 4 (1967)
p. 89 (S)

_____. <u>Garland of Stories</u>. Devon: Arthur Stockwell, [1960?].
*Forsaken/...And All the While Jamal Watched/Sakina, I Love
You Still!/Karma and the Kaieteur/Under the Banyan Tree/Hoof-
beats after Midnight (S)

_____. "Heritage," in Gora Singh's <u>Heritage</u> (P)

_____. <u>Hoofbeats at Midnight: A Play in One Act</u>. [type-
script] (D)

_____. "Jhaman Maraj," p. 6 <u>Heritage 2</u> (S)

_____. "Kanya-Daan (Gift of a Virgin)," p. 29 <u>Heritage 2</u> (P)

_____. "Karma and the Kaieteur," <u>Kaie</u> 1 (1965) p. 10 and 4
(1967) (S)

_____. <u>Roraima: A Radio Play</u>. winner of 1966 Demba Radio
Play Competition (D)

_____. "Sakina, I Love You Still!" p. 127 Seymour's <u>My Lovely
Native Land</u> (S)

_____. "Sardar Birbal Singh," <u>Kaie</u> 5 (1968) p. 31 (S)

_____. <u>Sound of Her Bells</u>. 1971 (D)

_____. <u>A White Camellia and a Blue Star</u>. [typescript] (D)

Singh, Sydney. "The Constant Perimeter," <u>Kyk-Over-Al</u> 18 (1954)
   p. 33 (C)

_____. "A Criticism of Contemporary Criticism," <u>Kyk-Over-Al</u>
   16 (1953) p. 155 (E)

Singham, Archie. <u>Three Cases of Constitutionalism and Cuckoo-
   Politics: Ceylon, British Guiana, and Grenada.</u> 1965. (F)

Smith, Arthur Goldwin, "Poem," <u>Kyk-Over-Al</u> 7 (1948) p. 5 also
   p. 48 Seymour's <u>Themes of Song</u> (P)

Smith, Jackie. <u>A Bitter Memory</u>. perf. Guyana 1968 (D)

Smith, James W. "Fear," <u>Kyk-Over-Al</u> 1 (1945) p. 9 (P)

_____. <u>Forgiveness. A Narrative Poem</u>. Georgetown: Argosy
   Co., 1944. (P)

_____. "A Letter to My Unborn Son," <u>Kyk-Over-Al</u> 2 (1946)
   p. 10 (P)

_____. "Poem," <u>Kyk-Over-Al</u> 4 (1947) p. 9 (P)

_____. "To a Dead Silk-Cotton Tree," <u>Kyk-Over-Al</u> 3 (1946)
   p. 9 (P)

_____. "To the Moon," <u>Kyk-Over-Al</u> 8 (1949) p. 5 (P)

_____. "To the Poets," <u>Kyk-Over-Al</u> 5 (1947) p. 13 (P)

_____. "Twilight," <u>Kyk-Over-Al</u> 6 (1948) p. 5 (P)

Smith, John. "A Slave's Day," p. 80 Seymour's <u>My Lovely Native
   Land</u> [excerpt from Rev. John Smith's Journal, recorded at
   Plantation Resouvenir, from 1817 to his death in 1824] (A,C)

_____. [cf. Wallbridge, (Rev.) E.A.--<u>The Demerara Martyr</u>]

Smith, Raymond T. <u>British Guiana</u>. London: Oxford, 1962. (C)

_____. <u>The Negro Family in British Guiana</u>. London: Routledge
   and Kegan Paul, 1956. (C)

Smith, Ricardo. <u>Miss Phoebe; or, Guyana Legend: A Play with
   Music in Three Acts</u>. perf. Georgetown for Independence Cele-
   brations 1966]from an earlier version: <u>Miss Phoebe: One
   Act Musical and Historical Play on Early Demerara</u> 1963] (D,Mu)

Smith, Walter O. [pseud. cf. P. Chattoram]

Sobers, Rose. "Imitation," <u>Chronicle Christmas Annual</u> (1957)
   p. 38 (S)

Sole, Samat. "White Boy," <u>Poet</u> 13, 1 (1972) p. 23 (P)

Solomon, G.P. "Kaieteur Express," <u>Christmas Tide</u> (1936) p. 28 (S)

_____. "The Scarlet Box," <u>Christmas Tide</u> (1934) p. 29 (S)

Sookhdeo, Jaikissoon. <u>Let Not the Great</u>. Devon: Arthur Stockwell, 1964. *Poetry/A Moonlight Memory/A Birthday Atmosphere
   (16th December)/A Birthday Atmosphere (15th May)/Be Humane/

A Christmas-New Year Wish/Farewell, Sister Dear/A Moment of Frustration/Lover's Imploration to Parents/Come My Friends/A Thought/Farewell! Love/Be Bold/A thought/Be Cultural/Oh Guyana/ It Burns My Heart/Lonely Mate/A Humble Entreaty/How Long Must I Wait?/When Two Lovers Depart/Give Me, My Love!/You Can't Stop Me From Loving You/I've Got Another/Age Doesn't Matter/ Forever True/Can't You Understand?/Why Do You Leave Me?/Happy Birthday/Bow in Thankfulness/Be Up/To My Darling Dear/My Inspiration (P)

Sparer, Joyce [Adler]. "The Art of Wilson Harris," New Beacon Reviews 1 (1968) p. 22 [ed. John LaRose] [orig. publ. as two articles in Georgetown Sunday Chronicle (Dec. 1967)] (E)

_____. "Attitudes Towards 'Race' in Guyanese Literature," Caribbean Studies 8, 2 (1968) p. 23 (E)

_____. "Carew--An Unfinished Search for Identity," Georgetown Sunday Chronicle (30 Apr. 1967) (E)

_____. "Melville and Harris: Poetic Imaginations Related in Their Response to the Modern World," p. 33 Maes-Jelinek's Commonwealth Literature and the Modern World (E)

_____. "Tumatumari and the Imagination of Wilson Harris," Journal of Commonwealth Literature 7 (1969) p. 20 (E)

_____. "Wilson Harris and Twentieth Century Man," New Letters 40, 1 (1973) p. 49 (E)

Speirs, (Rev.) James. Creole Life in British Guiana. [1901?]. (C

_____. The Proverbs of British Guiana with an Index of Principal Words, an Index of Subjects, and a Glossary. Demerara: Argosy Co., 1902. (F,L)

Stapie, Uncle. [pseud. cf. Evelyn-Moe, L.]

Steadman, Bret. "Autobiography," Chronicle Christmas Annual (1948 p. 16 (S)

Steele, Mark. "Night's Descent," Kyk-Over-Al 19 (1954) p. 54 (P)

Stephens, Herman A. "The Rain," p. 69 Cameron's Guianese Poetry... (P)

_____. "The Rat," Christmas Tide (1934) p. 36 (S)

_____. "The Way of the East," Christmas Tide (1936) p. 43 (S)

Stephenson, Elaine. Tamari: A Play in Three Acts. [typescript]

Stoby, Miles Sievewright. "After the Ball," New World (Fortnightly) 17 (1965) p. 12 (P)

_____. "Poem," New World (Fortnightly) 27/28 (1965) p. 21 (P)

_____. "Sketch for a Poem: Georgetown, February 1962," New World (Fortnightly) 29 (1965) p. 24 (P)

106

Stone, W.W. *Addenda p. 32/Bussing Big Gaff on the Bus p. 30/ Explaining to the Doctor p. 29/A Roadworker's Pause p. 34 Expression 2 (1967) (P)

_____. *The Police Are Investigating p. 28/There are No Shadows at Noontime p. 26/Woman in Labour p. 27 Expression 3½ (1967) (P)

Strong, Leonard. Gospel Reminiscences in the West Indies. London, 1845. (A)

Sukhnandan, Prasad. "Dawn of the Future," Kyk-Over-Al 13 (1951) p. 238 (S)

Sukhu, Leela. Scattered Leaves. Georgetown: Sheik Sadeek, 1968. [19 untitled "Thought-Forms"] (P)

The Sun. Georgetown, Saturdays; organ of U.F. (X)

The Sunday Graphic. Georgetown (X)

Swan, Michael. British Guiana the Land of Six Peoples. London: The Colonial Office. (C)

_____. "A Georgetown Day," p. 23 Seymour's My Lovely Native Land (C)

Sylvester, Otho. "The Batchie," Kyk-Over-Al 12 (1951) p. 140 (S)

T

T., H. Stray Thoughts. Demerara: Argosy Co., 1889. *Pro Rege et Patria/O Beautiful/Christmas/The Convict's Wife/Parted/ Where Stray My Thoughts/Green Fields/Sunshine/Silver Chimes/ The Snow/Father Land/The Cross/There's Not a Heart/Ring on Ye Bell/Memories/The Bells of Limerick/The Burial of John Hampden/ A Life's Picture/The Sea/Good-Bye/Good Night/Lines/Beautiful Dreams/There's No Song/Sea Voices/Flee as a Bird to your Mountain/Christmas Dreams/Liberty/Our Bark Rides On/Golden Dreams/Rest/No Cross No Crown/In Memoriam/What is Your Life/ A Requiem/Is Life Worth Living/Fifty Years Ago/Forgotten/The Old Colours/Time Works So Many Changes/Shadows/For Lack of Gold/A Nation's Sympathy/Sweet and Low/The Sabbath Day/Our Home/For Ever/Watching/Fading/Will You Love Me?/Auld Lang Syne/It is Sad to Know/'Tis Night at Sea/Sand Castles/I Love the Sea/A Prayer/By the River Side/Dawn/Farewell/On a Sleep- ing Infant/Mother/Christmas - 1886/The New Year, 1887/Gold/The Wreck/A Character/Hope/Friendship/The Evening Hour/To-Morrow/ Hope On, Hope On/Sail On, Sail On/The Petrel's Song/Livingstone/ Slumber on Sweetly/Sunny Memories/Lilies/A Memory/He Has Risen/ Mariner's Grave/Love Ever Love/The Night Has Come/Faith/Life/ Still in Sight/To the Old Year/Thought/Charity/Away from Thee/ Love/The Fisherman's Wife/'Tis The Last Ray/The New Year: 1899/ Victoria, 1899 (P)

Taharally, Kenneth. _Anthrophanies_. London: K. Taharally, 1972. Vol. I = _Nightwinds_; Vol. II = _Imagination's Family_ (P)

_____. [cf. Seymour, A.J.--"The Arts in Guyana"]

Taitt, Helen. "Arabesque," _Kyk-Over-Al_ 5 (1947) p. 10 and 19 (1954) p. 79 (P)

_____. "Evergone. With Thoughts of Edgar Mittelholzer," _New World_ 14 (1965) p. 2 (P)

_____. "Poem," _Kyk-Over-Al_ 7 (1948) p. 4 and 19 (1954) p. 75 (P

_____. "Somewhere," _Kyk-Over-Al_ 6 (1948) p. 3 (P)

Tamarack Review 14 (1960). [Toronto; a special West Indian literature issue] (J)

Tee--Van, Helen Danvrosch. _Red Howling Monkey_. London: Macmillan, 1926. (N?)

Telemaque, Harold M. _Scarlet_. Georgetown: Master Printery, 1953. (P?)

_____. "Turn the Page," _Kyk-Over-Al_ 11 (1950) p. 3 (P)

Ten-Pow, Rudolph C. *Mei Maiores--My Ancestors p. 28/Reality p. 30 _Kaie_ 8 (1971) (P)

_____. *Nightfall in Den Amstel p. 109/Sandy Babb Street Kitty p. 109 in Seymour's _New Writing in the Caribbean_ (P)

_____. "Raymond and Sonita," _Kaie_ 8 (1971) p. 44 (S)

Thieme, John, Annette Warren and George Cave. (eds.) _Anthology of West Indian Literature_. Georgetown: University of Guyana. (

Thomas, Noel R. "The Star of Israel," _Christmas Tide_ (1935) p. 12 (P)

Thomas, Pauline. [cf. McDonald, Ian--_Advance to the Brink_]

Thomas, Rudolph. "Message to the Black Man," _Kaie_ 10 (1973) p. 19 (P)

Thomasson, Frank. "Drama Training in British Guiana," _Kyk-Over-Al_ 25 (1959) p. 137 (E)

_____. [cf. Seymour, A.J.--"Greatness and Bitterness"]

_____. [cf. Seymour, A.J.--"Standards of Criticism"]

Thorne, Guy. "The Pantomime Cat," _Christmas Tide_ (1923) p. 33 (S)

Thorne, J.T. _Some Haphazard Notes of a Forty-Two Years' Residence in British Guiana_. Georgetown: Argosy, 1899. (A)

Thunder. East Coast Demerara, Guyana; began as weekly, continued as quarterly; organ of P.P.P. (X)

Timehri Magazine. The Journal of the Royal Agricultural and Commercial Society. British Guiana. [became _Timehri. The Journal of the Guyana Museum and Zoo_. Vol. 1, No. 1 was published June 1882. There is a cumulative index in No. 26 (Nov. 1944) listing both authors and subjects; subsequent issues of Timehri published these indices alternately] (J)

Ting-A-Kee, Laura. *Maybe p. 94/Strange p. 93/Waves p. 40 Kyk-Over-Al 19 (1954) (P)

Todd, Hugh. Poet's Song. Mackenzie, Linden, Guyana: author, 1973. *The Love I Found/My Love/My Lost Love/My Rosemary/My Darling Lesle/Silvia/The Damned Damsel/The Un-Wanted Messenger?/The Farmer/The City Street Scene/A Sonnet/The Wanderer/The Ant/The Gangasaka (House Lizard)/The Twa-Twa/The Mind/Depressed/Acquainted with Sorrow/Plea with Sorrow (P)

Tomas, J.L. (pseud.?) "The Things We Can't Control," Caribia (1949/50) p. 103 (S)

Townshend, Mitzie. "I Have Searched...," p. 37 Douglas' Guyana Drums (P)

Trotman, D.A.R. *Cave Cano p. 69/Essequibo p. 13/Music in the Dark p. 98/To Marian p. 68/To a Star p. 55 Kyk-Over-Al 19 (1954) (P)

_____. "Essequibo," p. 18 Seymour's Themes of Song also p. 16 Elma Seymour's Sun is a Shapely Fire (P)

_____. *Lotoyana p. 27/Stabroek p. 26/Sugar Cane Farmer p. 28 Kaie 3 (1966) (P)

_____. *Moon Thoughts p. 15/Nunc Dimittis p. 14/Polynika p. 16/Prologue to Sugar-Cane Farmer p. 17 Seymour's Magnet (P)

_____. Poems for My People. British Guiana: author, 1965. *Be Patient Now, My People/Asylum/Memento/Emancipation/A Rustic Thought/Caveat/May, 1963/Music in the Dark/Nunc Dimittis/Judgement/Night Image/The Hills of Zorg/Maguyana/Margery/Negligence/Stabroek/Lagos Morning/'Lines--On a Village Wedding'/Despair/Africa/Lotoyana/Prologue to 'Sugar-Cane Farmer'/Autumn/Moon Thought/Polynika (P)

_____. "Voices of the Grove," p. 21 Trotman's Voices of Guyana (P)

_____. (ed.) Voices of Guyana. Georgetown: Sheik Sadeek, 1968. (P)

Trotz, Marilyn. "French Caribbean Literature," Kaie 11 (1973) p. 85 (E)

Tudor, Cameron. "Mr. Pipson's Revenge," Chronicle Christmas Annual (1949) p. 15 (S)

Tulloch, Cecil M. *A Dream p. 66/My Jewel p. 67 Kyk-Over-Al 19 (1954) (P)

_____. *Epitaph to My Father p. 25/Guyana p. 25/Guyana--Revealed p. 24/I Love You p. 24/You p. 24 Kaie 5 (1968) (P)

U

Uchlein, C.T. "Where the Fires are not Quenched," <u>Kyk-Over-Al</u> 18 (1954) p. 24 (S)

Undine. "The Broken Promise," <u>Christmas Tide</u> (1934) p. 30 (S)

A Uniao Portuguêza. [Archives 1889-1890 incomplete] (X)

V

Valz, Oliver Mortimer. "Bitter Waters," <u>Christmas Tide</u> (1949) p. 46 (S)

Van Berkel, Adriaan. <u>Travels in South America Between the Ber-bice and Essequibo Rivers, and in Surinam 1670-1689.</u> George-town: Daily Chronicle, 1941. [Guiana Edition transl. and ed. 1925 by Walter E. Roth. Orig. publ. Amsterdam, 1695, this is the first book to describe the area of what is now Guyana] (A,T)

Vanier, E.G. "He Did What They Wanted," <u>Christmas Tide</u> (1936) p. 65 (S)

Van Sertima, Ivan Gladstone. "Black Prince," p. 267 Seymour's <u>New Writing in the Caribbean</u> (S)

_____. <u>Caribbean Writers, Critical Essays</u>. London: New Beacon, 1968; New York: Panther, 1971. (Cr)

_____. "Darkened the Diamond," <u>Kyk-Over-Al</u> 24 (1958) p. 49 (P)

_____. "The Hidden Ocean," <u>Kyk-Over-Al</u> 19 (1954) p. 86 (P)

_____. "If I Could Speak," <u>Kyk-Over-Al</u> 20 (1955) p. 145 (P)

_____. "Life and Death (Dialogue on Man's Mortality and Sig-nificance)", <u>Kyk-Over-Al</u> 23 (1958) p. 35 (P)

_____. "Life's Mountain," <u>Kyk-Over-Al</u> 19 (1954) p. 87 (P)

_____. "The Lost and the Lonely," <u>Kyk-Over-Al</u> 26 (1959) p. 36 ["from a novel in progress"] (S)

_____. "The Lost Ones," <u>Kaie</u> 4 (1967) p. 79 also p. 45 Elma Seymour's <u>Sun is a Shapely Fire</u> (P)

_____. "Menageria," <u>Poet</u> 13, 1 (1972) p. 19 also <u>Kaie</u> 4 (1967) p. 78 also p. 40 Salkey's <u>Breaklight</u> (P)

_____. "Mirage," Kyk-Over-Al 27 (1960) p. 67 (P)

_____. "Muse Without Music," Kyk-Over-Al 23 (1958) p. 9 (P)

_____. "Poem for Princess Margaret," Kyk-Over-Al 23 (1958)
p. 1 (P)

_____. River and the Wall. British Guiana: Master Printery,
1958. [Miniature Poet Series] *Muse Without Music/Like a
Lost Drop/Menagerie/For This I Came/Samadhi/The River and the
Wall/The Unfinished Symphony/Hunting for the Whale/The Lost
Ones/Some Breath of Magic (a Fragment)/Volcano (P)

_____. "The Tide of Time," Kyk-Over-Al 19 (1954) p. 88 (P)

_____. "Volcano," Kyk-Over-Al 23 (1958) p. 11 also p. 41
Salkey's Breaklight (P)

_____. "Will," Kyk-Over-Al 19 (1954) p. 85 also p. 47
Seymour's Themes of Song (P)

Van Sertima, J. Among the Common People of British Guiana.
Georgetown, Demerara: C.K. Jardine, 1897. [reprinted in
book form from articles in the Daily Chronicle] *Morning/
Breakfast/Night/Dress/Sickness/Death and After/The Funeral/
Rebecca Before and After the Royal Commissioners/Rebecca on
Social Questions/Rebecca's Ball/The Combined Court: Rebecca's
Reflections/The Cricket Carnival/Sarah's Herb-Woman/Rebecca's
Marriage (C)

_____. The Creole Tongue of British Guiana. New Amsterdam,
Berbice, 1905. (includes excerpts of western "classics"
transl. into Creolese] (Cr,L)

_____. Scenes and Sketches. Georgetown, 1899. [reprints in
book form of pieces appearing in the Argosy] *'Ole Mudda
Spenca'/Police Court Sketches/Reminiscences of Queen's College/
A Sunday Morning/The Gold-Digger--in Urbe/The Gold-Digger--In
Silvis/Our Street Boys/The Coolie Porter/The Policeman/The
Washerwoman/The Charms of the Chinese Chéfa/Christmas in
Georgetown/An Incurable Petition/In the Presence of the Dead/
The Funeral (C)

Van Sertima, Sheila. Admit Joe. broadcast History and Culture
Week 1964 (D)

_____. It's Brickdam! Kyk-Over-Al 25 (1959) p. 139 (D)

_____. "Under the Sun," Chronicle Christmas Annual (1958)
p. 21 (S)

Veecock, J. Falstaff: A Comedy. 1893. (D)

_____. "Notes on Legends of British Guiana," West Indian
Quarterly Vol. 3 (July 1887) p. 306 (F,Cr)

Veecock, Walter J. [same as Veecock, J. - above?] 'Phileron':
The Tragedy of a Poet Soul, and a Few Other Fragments.
Edinburgh: J. and W. Meade, 1896. *Poems: Summer Hours/Youth's

Answer/True Love/Heart-Throb/Angel Love/Moon-Dream/A Child's
Prayer/Even-Thought/Song/A Highland Sungleam/Autumn/A Prayer/
Longings/Yearnings/Stanzas/Spring Throbbings; Drama: Phileron
(P,D)

Veness, W.T. May Morley and Other Fugitive Pieces. 1856. (S?)

Vidyahanand, George. *Fish Koker p. 2/Lonely Dam p. 14 Monar's
Poems for Guyanese Children (P)

Vieira, Philip. "Forest Child," Chronicle Christmas Annual
(1949) p. 35 (S)

Voices. [Ed. by Clifford Sealy, Port of Spain, Trinidad] (J)

Vojáka, Knihovna. Černošská: Světová Antologie. Praha: Nase
Vojsko, 1958. (P)

W

W., H.W. Georgetown Vignettes. 1917. (E?)

Waby, (Mrs.) E.F. "That Second Swizzle," Christmas Tide (1921)
p. 12 (S)

Waites, J. Arthur. "Is There a West Indian Culture?" Kyk-Over-Al
9 (1949) p. 5 (E)

Wallace, Evelyn. The Moco Moco Tree (An Ol' Higue Story).
Georgetown: Guyana Ministry of Education, 1973. (S,F)

Wallbridge, (Rev.) Edwin A. The Demerara Martyr. Georgetown:
Daily Chronicle, 1943. [orig. 1848; memoirs of Rev. John
Smith] (A)

Wallerson, Oscar. That I May Reach You: Poems by Oscar Waller-
son. Mackenzie (Linden), Guyana: Linden Art Group, 1973.
*Fight, My Beloved Country/And the Spirit Moves/Distant Drums/
My Heritage/A Destiny to Mould/Streets/And He Coloured Me
Black/Roraima/Youth/Peace Not Conflict/That I May Reach You (P)

Walmsley, Anne. (comp.) The Sun's Eye: West Indian Writing for
Young Readers. London: Longman, 1968. (Y)

Warren, Annette. "Face Tapestry," New World (Fortnightly) 38
(1966) p. 19 also p. 112 Searwar's Co-Operative Republic (P)

_____. "Motorcycle Monomaniac," New World (Fortnightly) 38
(1966) p. 20 (P)

_____. "North Savannah," New World (Fortnightly) 42 (1966)
p. 24 (P)

_____. "Ten Themes," Kaie 5 (1968) p. 5 [ten connected
poems] (P)

Waruk, Kona. [pseud. cf. Harris, Wilson: <u>Eternity to Season</u> (1952 edn.), and <u>Fetish</u>]

<u>Watchman</u>. [Archives 1871-1879 incomplete] (X)

Watson, Ivan. <u>To Gain a Land (A Collection of Poems)</u>. Georgetown, 197-? *In Quest of Shadows/At the House of the Talking Feet/Through Twilight/Just Memory/Just People/Of Dying/In the Land of the Living/I am Pushing/Cuffy/Some Passion/Just a Thought/On a Journey to the Mind/A Journey Into the Outer Region of the Mind/A Journey Into the Inner Region of the Mind/A Reminder/Eyes Ahead/To Meet a Land/To Gain a Land/ From Home: With Love (P)

Wayfarer. (pseud.) "Mail Day," <u>Christmas Tide</u> (1923) p. 15 (S)

Webber, A.R.F. <u>A Centenary History and Handbook of British Guiana</u>. Georgetown: Argosy, 1931. (C)

_____. <u>Glints from an Anvil: Being Lines of a Song</u>. Georgetown: Daily Chronicle, 1918. (P)

_____. *Guiana! p. 180/Peace or War p. 169/When I Depart p. 170 Cameron's <u>Guianese Poetry...</u> (P)

_____. <u>Those that Be in Bondage: A Tale of East Indian Indentures and Sunlit Western Water</u>. Georgetown: Daily Chronicle, 1917. [appeared orig. in serial form] (N)

<u>Week End Post and Sunday Argosy</u>. Georgetown, Sundays. (X)

<u>The Weekly Argosy</u>. [Archives 1907-1909 incomplete] (X)

Welch, Ivan. "Kaietuk," <u>Kyk-Over-Al</u> 19 (1954) p. 26 (P)

Welcome, Doris. "Life's Jewels," <u>Chronicle Christmas Annual</u> (1946) p. 28 (P)

Westmaas, David H. "The Arms and Legs of the Law," <u>Chronicle Christmas Annual</u> (1958) p. 8 (S)

_____. "Brenda on the Beam," <u>Chronicle Christmas Annual</u> (1955) p. 26 (S)

_____. <u>The Harvesters: A Play in the Vernacular in Three Scenes</u>. (D)

_____. "Kaiteur's Revenge," <u>Christmas Tide</u> (1948) p. 32 (S)

_____. <u>Old Suit, New Cloth: A Comedy</u>. [typescript] (D)

_____. "On Writing Creolese," <u>Kyk-Over-Al</u> 7 (1948) p. 16 (E)

Westmaas, Leonard A. "Command Performance," <u>Chronicle Christmas Annual</u> (1956) p. 4 (S)

_____. "The Idiots," <u>Chronicle Christmas Annual</u> (1952) p. 4 (S)

_____. "Rendezvous," <u>Chronicle Christmas Annual</u> (1954) p. 9 (S)

_____. "That Strain Again," <u>Chronicle Christmas Annual</u> (1953) p. 36 (S)

Wharton, Hugh. <u>Some Guianese Short Stories</u>. Georgetown: At Last
    Publishing Agency, 1963. (S)

Wharton, Verona. "Jasmin's Dream," <u>Chronicle Christmas Annual</u>
    (1959) p. 28 (S)

White, Lloyd B. <u>Sunset of Light; or, Vision Over Guiana: A Play
    in Two Acts</u>. [typescript] (D)

White, Stanley Hamilcar. "Belshazzar," <u>Kyk-Over-Al</u> 5 (1947)
    p. 11 [fragment of poem] (P)

_____. "Nebuchadnezzar," <u>Kyk-Over-Al</u> 1 (1945) p. 8 [fragment
    of the poem] (P)

_____. "Star of Eve," <u>Kyk-Over-Al</u> 6 (1948) p. 5 and 19 (1954)
    p. 57 also p. 29 Seymour's <u>Themes of Song</u> (P)

White, (Rev.) Walter G. "Kanaima's Call," <u>Chronicle Christmas
    Annual</u> (1928) (S)

Wilburn, Mary N. "The Timehri Murals," <u>Kaie</u> 8 (1971) p. 74 (S)

Williams, Denis. "Art and Society," <u>Kaie</u> 11 (1973) p. 100 [paper
    delivered at Carifesta, 1972] (E)

_____. <u>Giglioli in Guyana 1922-1972</u>. Georgetown: National
    History and Arts Council, 1973. [No. 1 in the Library of
    Biography] (B)

_____. "Guiana Today," <u>Kyk-Over-Al</u> 9 (1949) p. 9 (E)

_____. "Hamilton of the Sudan," <u>Kyk-Over-Al</u> 27 (1960) p. 87 (E)

_____. <u>Image and Idea in the Arts of Guyana</u>. Georgetown:
    National History and Arts Council, 1969. [text of Edgar
    Mittelholzer Memorial Lectures] (E)

_____. "A Long Long Pause," p. 218 Salkey's <u>Stories from the
    Caribbean</u> (S)

_____. <u>Other Leopards</u>. London: Hutchinson, 1963. (N)

_____. "Other Leopards," p. 235 Dathorne's <u>Caribbean Narra-
    tive</u> (N-e)

_____. "Sperm of God," p. 301 Seymour's <u>New Writing in the
    Caribbean</u> [extract] (S)

_____. <u>The Third Temptation: A Novel</u>. London: Calder and
    Boyars, 1968. (N)

_____. [cf. Seymour, A.J.--"An Exchange of Letters"]

Williams, (Dr.) Frank. [cf. Seymour, A.J.--"Is There a West
    Indian Way of Life?"]

Williams, Milton, "The Agony of Icarus (Prays to the Muse),"
    <u>Kyk-Over-Al</u> 28 (1961) p. 179 (P)

_____. *At the Moment p. 106/Iron Punts Laden with Cane
    p. 30/Pray for Rain p. 180 Salkey's <u>Breaklight</u> (P)

114

_____. "Careful Brother," Kyk-Over-Al 24 (1958) p. 49 (P)

_____. *Here There's a War On p. 5/Iron Punts Laden with Cane p. 6/Pray for Rain p. 6/Sometimes a Man p. 3 Kyk-Over-Al 23 (1958) (P)

_____. "I Wifeless," Kaie 4 (1967) p. 80 also Kyk-Over-Al 23 (1958) p. 3 (P)

_____. "Icarus," Kyk-Over-Al 28 (1961) p. 178 (P)

_____. "Iron Punts Laden with Cane," Poet 13, 1 (1972) p. 24 also p. 79 Seymour's My Lovely Native Land (P)

_____. "New Songs," Kaie 2 (1966) p. 45 (P)

_____. "Oh! Prahalad Dedicated Day," Kaie 4 (1967) p. 80 also Kyk-Over-Al 23 (1958) p. 5 also p. 104 Searwar's Co-Operative Republic (P)

_____. "Poems. For P.V.S." Kyk-Over-Al 27 (1960) p. 70 (P)

_____. "Poet in a Slave Arena," Kyk-Over-Al 26 (1959) p. 47 (E)

_____. Pray for Rain. British Guiana, 1958. [Miniature Poet Series] *Pray for Rain/Iron Punts Laden with Cane/Sometimes a Man/Here There's a War On/Oh! Prahalad Dedicated Day/I Wifeless/Roots--1/Roots (ii)/Saturday Night/Between Your Thighs/At the Moment/Slowly Over the Face (P)

_____. "Sometimes a Man," Poet 13, 1 (1972) p. 24 (P)

_____. "Tristram (Son of Sorrow)," Kyk-Over-Al 26 (1959) p. 8 (P)

Williams, Monty. "To Martin Carter," GISRA 5, 4 (1974) p. 64 (P)

Williams, N. *An Odi Et Amo p. 9/Undone p. 8 Expression 4 (1968) (P)

_____. "The Rebirth of Geoffrey Sinclair," Savacou 3/4 (1971) p. 160 (S)

_____ and M. Michael Drepaul. (eds.) Expression 2. Georgetown: the editors, 1967. ["An independent literary magazine, designed to encourage and expose creative writing"] (J)

_____. (eds.) Expression 3½. Georgetown: the editors, 1967.(J)

_____. [cf. Cotton, Brian--Expression I]

Williams, Walter. The Flames Came Back. Georgetown: Daily Chronicle. [narrative poem] (P)

_____. "The Seventh Veil," Kyk-Over-Al 3 (1946) p. 11 (P)

_____. "These are the Men," Chronicle Christmas Annual (1948) p. 35 (P)

Wills, S.E. 50 Local Lyrics. (P)

_____. *Before and After p. 133/Christmas in the Tropics p. 163/ That Was Then p. 159/A Tribute to the Memory of J.S. McArthur p. 124 Cameron's Guianese Poetry... (P)

Wilson, A. Gaylord. "Hen-Pecked Hero," <u>Chronicle Christmas Annual</u> (1955) p. 30 (S)

Wilson, Donald G. (ed.) <u>New Ships. An Anthology of West Indian Poems for Secondary Schools</u>. Kingston: Savacou Publication, 1971 (P)

Wilson, T-Bone. "Tarringdale Leaps," <u>Savacou</u> 9/10 (1974) p. 86 (P)

Winter, Phil H. "An Acrostic," <u>New Nation</u> (Guyana) (Feb. 1973) p. 15 (P)

_____. <u>Earth Has No Place</u>. Ilfracombe, Devon: A.H. Stockwell, 1970. *It's Different/I Was Born Again/I Mourn My Life/Little Babe/It is Here/Darkened Cloud/Earthly Pain/Be Kind to Me/ Another Day/Myriad's Nest/The Seeds I Cherish/Melancholy Dazed/ The Stranger/Different Way/The Silent Stream/Changing Years/ The Heavens Mourn/Cascading Voices/Realisable Folly/From the Dust/Melon Madness/Hurried Moments/Life to Death/A Minute Late/ My Brother's Paradise/Quickly/A Tool/How Long/Lives Far Away/ Glowing Tears (P)

_____. "How Long," Georgetown <u>Sunday Graphic</u> (12 Mar. 1972) p. 4 (P)

_____. *I Was Born Again p. 8/Unwanted Life p. 8 Georgetown <u>Sunday Graphic</u> (14 Jan. 1973) (P)

_____. "It is Here," p. 58 <u>A New Guyana</u> (P)

_____. *An Oven/The Sea/Yesterday broadcast Guyana Broadcasting Service 1971 (P)

_____. *Realisable Folly/The Seeds I Cherish <u>London Anthology</u>. London: Avon, 1968. (P)

Winzh, Joel. "Waiting," <u>Expression 4</u> (1968) p. 5 (P)

Wishart, C.C. "A Link with the Old Colonial Past," <u>Chronicle Christmas Annual</u> (1967) p. 79 (P)

Wishart, Nellie. "Behaviour Patterns," Georgetown <u>Daily Chronicle</u> [from Feb. 1974 onwards, in serial form: 15 stories published with analyses] (S,Cr)

_____. "The Imposter," <u>Chronicle Christmas Annual</u> (1960) p. 21 (S)

_____. "Misfortune's Daughter," Georgetown <u>Daily Chronicle</u> (Dec. 1959) (S)

_____. "My Dream," Georgetown <u>Daily Chronicle</u> (Feb. 1970) (P)

_____. "No Return Passage," Georgetown <u>Daily Argosy</u> (Dec. 1959) (S)

Woods, Mary. [cf. Seymour, A.J.--"The Arts in Guiana"]

Woodsley, H. Austin. [pseud. cf. Mittelholzer, Edgar--<u>Mad Mac Mullochs</u>]

Working Man. [Archives 1872] (X)

World Literature Written in English. [continues CBCL; began publ. 1962; twice-yearly from Univ. of Texas at Arlington; bibliographies, articles, interviews, reviews] (J)

"Writers of the Caribbean, 1. Master Pens of British Guiana," Flamingo (London) 1, 8 (1962) p. 34. (E)

Wynter, Sylvia. (adapter) Black Midas. London: Longmans, 1970. [adaptation for children of Jan Carew's novel Black Midas] (N)

_____. [cf. Carew, Jan--The University of Hunger]

Y

Y., J.A.E. [cf. Seymour, A.J.--"Greatness and Bitterness"]

Yardan, Shana. "Earth is Brown," p. 113 Seymour's New Writing in the Caribbean (P)

_____. *Ever Waiting p. 11/Places p. 15/Renewal p. 16 Kaie 10 (1973) (P)

_____. *Illusion p. 43/Reaching Out p. 45 Douglas' Guyana Drums (P)

Yhap, Kathleen A. "A Bush Tale," Christmas Tide (1950) p. 46 (S)

York, Andrew. [pseud. cf. Nicole, Christopher]

Young, Allan. [cf. Seymour, A.J.--"The Arts in Guyana"]

ROBERT E. McDOWELL, Professor of English at the University of Texas, Arlington, has for several years edited the journal **World Literature Written in English** for English 12 of the Modern Language Association. Dr. McDowell has traveled and studied in India, Africa, and the West Indies, and is well known for his writing on Commonwealth literatures. Most recently, he was Fulbright/Hays Lecturer at the University of Guyana.

SABLE PUBLISHING CORPORATION

P. O. BOX 788   ARLINGTON, TEXAS 76010

$10